NIPPLES ON MY

CW01619558

By Graham and Debra Robertson

MAPLE CREEK MEDIA
Hampstead ◊ Maryland ◊ USA

Printed in the United States of America

ISBN-13: 9781942914303
ISBN-10: 194291430X

MAPLE CREEK MEDIA

P.O. Box 624
Hampstead, MD 21074
Toll-Free Phone: 1-877-866-8820
Toll-Free Fax: 1-877-778-3756
Email: info@maplecreekmedia.com
Website: www.maplecreekmedia.com

FORWARD

Hi, and welcome to our world. Let me give you some information up front about this book.

It is a snapshot of our years in the sheep business and, at times, may be a little graphic for some, disagreed with by others, but generally the way things are and have been over the years.

It is not being written to teach people how to raise sheep, encourage, discourage, as a guide, or any other purpose than to provide an insight to what we have experienced as have many others that raise and deal with sheep.

I can only hope it gives you as large a smile as we have had over the years and perhaps a damp eye.

We have always endeavored to treat animals with care and respect, to the best of our capacity, and enjoy doing it.

I owe a large debt of gratitude to my loving wife, Debi, and my son, George, for all their assistance and patience over the years, and for putting up with me and my sheep, or as Debi likes to call them, "My ladies."

CONTENTS

IN THE BEGINNING

In the beginning, He looked down and saw that man had a need for meat at on his table when he was hungry, wool to clothe him when he was cold, milk for his cheese, and something to count when he lacked sleep. Thus, sheep were created.

I must admit up front that I never aspired to be in the sheep business, or be a shepherd or a farmer, for that matter. When growing up if someone told me someday I would own a farm and raise sheep, I would have told them to have their sanity checked!

Our lives and our paths often come under the control of others. I came to Maryland courtesy of the United States Army. Upon separation, I found Maryland was as good a place as any to stay. Close enough to where my family had relocated in northern New Jersey, but far enough away to be on my own.

My previous place in Maryland was a forty-acre farm where I raised and boarded horses. The farm and buildings dated back to the Civil War era with little improvement. I would have almost expected to see rebel cavalry riding across my field and several minor battles were fought nearby. It would have been quite in character with the physical farm. At the time it was purchased, one might think the place was abandoned. Overgrown fields and a gutted farmhouse…you get the picture.

Nipples On My Knee

There was an occasion when someone came by to visit the previous farm, when I was out in the field plowing, or trying to figure out how to do so.

Long time farmers always make it look so simple. Drive tractor, drop plow, plow. The reality is that it takes a while to master. My guest remarked about how I was a “real” farmer. Yep, was the reply, came from a long line of farmers. The truth be known, I was born and raised in Manhattan in New York City. The closest I came to dirt was Central Park. If there was any farming background, it was unknown to me.

When mentioning to people that we own a small farm, they would usually reply, “That’s great!” No offense, but what always came to mind was that this idiot has never owned, lived, or been on a farm.

Reality check…

Having a farm is rewarding, but is also a lot of hard work. Animals do not work 9 to 5 with weekends off. They do not celebrate Christmas. They expect to be taken care of and fed in all types of weather, no matter how cold, no matter how hot, how wet, the same as any other day.

My introduction to sheep came through my previous wife who decided to try raising sheep. She purchased five bred Southdown ewes. And the adventure started. The sheep were put in the pasture across the road from the main farm and there was a partly filled-in conduit, about two feet in diameter, under the road between the two pastures. Sure enough, my wife came to me, in a panic, because one of her ewes had crawled into it and had gotten stuck.

I’m a claustrophobic and I steadfastly refused to crawl in to rescue her ewe. Our farmer friend agreed to the task and was able to drag her out by the rear legs. Several days later, another one repeated the escape attempt. I still refused to rescue it and said that as far as I was concerned, she could stay in there until she died. I was a horseman, not a shepherd. As luck would have it, we had a gully-washer that washed her out of the conduit, unharmed.

After the lambs went to auction and only brought in around ten dollars a piece, it showed that the operation was not financially viable, and the sheep went to auction.

Being the type person who has always tried to stay on top of things, I found myself often working sixteen hours a day, seven days a week, and that included working full-time off the farm. I would come home and go back to work.

It took several years until one day the light bulb lit. The realization came to me that no matter how hard I worked, I could never get ahead of the work. The best I could hope for was to break even. After eleven years at it, I called it quits. I sold that farm, bought a rancher and went back to living the so-called normal life.

Well, it came to pass that I had an opportunity to purchase a parcel of farmland from an old friend at a great price. She was a realtor and had purchased a large farm from an estate. I had my choice of several parcels, but picked one that had about three acres with a stream.

It was bottomland around a stream. Having been flooded out on my previous farm, I asked if the property could be enlarged. The friend from whom I was buying this said "Sure, mark where you wish the property line to be." They would have the plat changed. I proceeded to do the survey with my rifle and telescopic site, a pack of metal stakes and a sledgehammer. It came out to be eight acres. Much better!

I contracted with a builder I knew from dealings in the past and decided on what style and where to site the house. I chose a spot on the top of a hill at the highest corner of the property.

The property is still quite rural and the surrounding properties are mostly farmland. The house has the kind of semi-isolation in which you can go outside naked and no one would see you, or care if you were. It meets my idea of perfection. Another deciding factor was that I was about to become a daddy for the first time at the ripe old age of fifty. Growing up on a farm is, in my humble opinion, a great environment for a child. They learn the value of a day's work. Their knowledge of sex is graphically portrayed. Life's lessons about reproduction, birth and death are part of the everyday scene.

It was a short drive to the town. We were able to sit on the front porch and listen to the birds and watch the deer graze in the next pasture. It was from the madding crowd. Life was good!

From previous lessons learned about streams, it made sense to build as high and as far above the stream as was practical. No matter how small and placid the little stream looks (small enough to leap across), I learned of the power that can come with heavy rains. The previous farm sat along the road in a valley. The valley was probably about a quarter of a mile across, and dead flat. A stream that ran through the far side was normally about six feet across and maybe six inches deep. Then a hurricane came. No one would have ever convinced me that there was any risk of a flood. At the peak, the water was up to six or eight feet deep across the entire valley. The fortunate part was the only damage to the house was a flooded basement. About three AM, the house was an island surrounded by a flowing river. I vowed that I would never live on the bottom again, always on a hill. Another of life's lessons learned.

I still have a small Ford tractor and mower deck from the

previous farm. I just couldn't bear to part with it as we were both about the same age. Small tractors are much in demand from people who have a small piece of property or farmette. An interesting side note: Even though the tractor is fifty years old, it could sell for four or five times what it cost brand new. It amazes me to see how many of these models are still around and in use today. Living up a private farm lane, when you get snowed in, you dig your own way out!

Now, while this may be painting a picture most people would love, there also comes a certain responsibility to maintain. You learn how quickly the grass and weeds can grow. Farmland is not exactly your lawn. The property had previously been used partly as a pasture for a beef operation and partly as a cornfield and had been fallow for several years. So, one of the farmers' scourges, primrose, had started to take over. The ironic part, as I remember, was that years ago the government had actually encouraged farmers to plant this stuff. They extolled the virtue of how it made great livestock barriers, made a colorful display of flowers and provided food for wild birds with its seeds. The problem is the seeds. They tend to pass through the birds, which is why it mainly grows along fences where they "plant and distribute" them. If you don't know what it is, think of barbed wire with leaves and pretty little white flowers. Nasty stuff with a tenacious will to live. In places, it was as much as ten feet tall and resembled steel wool. If they wish to surround prisons so escape is unlikely, forget barbed wire and plant primrose. It would take an elephant or a rhino with a tough hide to get through. It shouldn't take a rocket scientist to figure that after spending hours a month on a tractor with a mower trying to keep up with it, there must be a better solution.

The first issue was fences. Although some of the old wood

fences were still in place, more were needed to completely enclose the new property boundaries. I borrowed a tractor with a front bucket loader from a farmer up the road and began fencing. I learned a very valuable shortcut to do fencing. In the spring, when the ground is soft, you need one person (who trusts you completely) to hold the post upright, and then push the post into the ground with the tractor's bucket. The trust part comes into play because the person holding the post is standing under the bucket. (Oh, the stupid things we do without thinking of the consequences!) If the ground is resilient, you need to raise the bucket and bring it down to pound the post into the ground. On one post I almost made a post out of Debi. If I had been a split second slower reversing the bucket, it might possibly have killed her! I like to think that she never knew how close she came to injury or death. So stupid!

When the fences were up, the next order of business was to create a shelter. Nothing fancy, it was an 8 x 24 feet, three wall structure with a metal roof. It faced the wood line to provide a windbreak.

The original occupants were two horses that were boarded at the previous farm. I moved them in as soon as the structure and fencing were completed. Now, two horses are neat and fun to ride but don't make a serious dent in the amount of grass we were starting to get in the pasture.

When time permitted, I started work on a small barn. Picture a farm barn built to a scale of about four inches to the foot. T111 plywood siding that resembles sawn wood, painted barn red (of course), and had a gambrel metal roof. It had an upstairs for hay storage, and the first floor had a wide center aisle way and four horse stalls as I was considering breeding horses again. After some serious thought, I think I must have been out of my mind. I decided to get some sheep to help keep the grass down. I didn't know much about them. Heck, what's to know? I had bred and raised thoroughbred racehorses so sheep should be a "piece of cake." Stupid me again! The local pet stores do not have sheep in stock, so I had to look elsewhere.

The town I live in still has a livestock auction, held on Tuesday evenings, so off I went. I registered and sat in the gallery above the small ring where they display the animals being sold. I was probably trying to look like the rest of the farmers and people, even though I lacked bib coveralls and ball cap.

There is an illuminated sign above the auctioneer that displays the weight of the animal as they drive them through a scale before the ring. If you have attended an auction, the pace is fast and the auctioneer frequently speaks in a fast spiel that you need to de-cipher. The stock is run through at the rate of about one every thirty seconds to a minute, leaving little time to think and decide. If one was to stop and think for a minute, you might miss out. The idea, you realize later, is to go into the holding pens before and check the animals in which you may be interested in owning. Kick the tires, so to speak. Then get the number that is pasted on their back and write it down. They do not announce these numbers so speed-reading in the ring is essential. They ran a black face ewe into the ring and I put in a few bids, I won the bid. You hold up your card to the auctioneer with a number given to you when you register.

I'm in the sheep business and sheep like company, being flock animals, so I bought a second ewe. Not being fully prepared to be in the sheep business, I went home and hooked up my horse trailer, and proudly came back to pick up my stock. I guess, in hindsight, it was an impulse purchase. I drove home, pulled down into the pasture, and unloaded my new ladies in their new home. They proceeded to walk around the pasture and got familiar with the surroundings and settled in. This is going to be easy.

Being a family operation we decided to name our new arrivals. I named the first ewe, Debi II (which bugged Debi somewhat), and she decided to name the current and future ewes after states. Hence, the other one became known as 'Alabama'. We later started to name the offspring of the states after the capitals or major cities. We got away from this in later years, choosing names for them on whatever came to mind. We chose names that were suggested by visiting children or children in our home schooling group.

I did not know anything about either of these ewes. It was only through the luck of the draw that both were healthy and more importantly, bred. We now know that Alabama had enough years on her for Medicaid. She did not have a full set of eight teeth, which "The Book" infers is how you can get an idea of their age. I laugh when I look through my old notes where I had logged that she had six teeth on one side and none on the other. "The Book" says that adult sheep should have eight. People who know sheep will be laughing at this point. Sheep don't have any upper teeth…just bare gums. The learning curve had started.

Being elated with my obvious success, I returned the next week to see about getting more ewes. I really began to feel a little foolish when I came to the shocking realization that the previous week I had paid about twice the going price for the two that I had purchased. I felt like a rube that had just rolled off of a turnip truck. It was just another item in the learning curve. Get to know the market. Learn what the going price is before you buy. It did turn out well as both of the original "ladies" went on to produce several good crops of lambs for us.

That evening yielded five more "ladies", as Debi prefers. Four more states were added to our country farm. The fifth one, Debi eventually named Spock, due to her face color. Did I mention that Debi is a Trekkie?

And then came the days of the nervous shepherd, as we waited for the big event...our first lambs. I was the one who was practically living with the ewe. We had her in one of the horse stalls, and I waited. And waited. And waited. Like a pacing father in the delivery room. This is in the winter, naturally, and of course, very cold.

And then, wow! Look at that! She gave birth to our first lamb. I'm sure I was more excited than she was, as it's likely she had done it before. When the second one appeared, there was a problem. It was a sac lamb. The birth sac did not break during delivery. The lamb comes out looking like a sausage. Once the cord breaks, the lamb is on its own. If the sac does not get removed quickly, the lamb can't breathe. I was in somewhat of a panic at that point. I quickly peeled the sac off the lamb. And then, per the book, I proceeded to swing the lamb by its rear legs in order to clear the passages of fluid. They do point out to make sure you do not swing the lamb into anything and harm it. Swinging it into a wall will not increase its chance to survive. The lamb choked a few times, started shaking its head. Success! I'm a proud foster parent. Next hurtle, making sure that they nurse.

By this time, I was chilled to the bone. I couldn't leave them until I was sure the lambs had their first meal, which is critical for survival. The first meal is a mixture of milk and colostrum. This thick, nutrient rich mixture, which resembles condensed milk, provides an initial boost of energy and a boost to for the lamb's immune system from the ewe.

Will you lambs please find the tit and nurse so I can go back to the house and warm up? No, no, wrong end! There is nothing to feed you on her neck. Try again. The front shoulders do not milk either. Well, after what seemed like days, but was probably more like half an hour, they were able to connect with the mother ship and fuel up. The little tails wag a mile a minute, a sign that fuel is being delivered and received life is good.

Alabama proved to be the bad girl of the time. She had the habit of testing fences, either pushing through or under to eat. This bugged Debi, who one time was heard to remark, “She will be the first to go.” Just when things were looking bad for her, she delivers our first set of triplets. The largest of the three was a coal black ewe. Debi promptly named kiwi black shoe polish, or as she subsequently became known, kiwi. One of the other littermates had a rather unusual black and white face and became gypsy. The third lamb, a ram, was very small, the runt of the litter. He was not doing very well, and required supplementation. That week I had a company affair to attend in Hershey Pa, and being that we were supplementing him, the lamb went with us. Probably the first time the hotel had a lamb in one of its rooms. We quietly snuck it in hidden in a cardboard box. It was not strong enough to make any noise, thus the plot went unheralded. Sad to say, our best efforts were in vain. He died that day. Both of her other lambs became part of our flock, as we were in the building phase. We pretty much were keeping any ewe lambs, though today, we would be more selective. Both turned out to be very productive members of our starting flock.

Another ewe, Texas, who became better known as bulldog, due to her course head, and face like a bulldog, lambed. On the second day, we found her down, and close to death. Panic time again. Not being able to rise to her feet, there was no way she would be able to nurse her two lambs. Thus begins our first experience with bottle lambs. It was back to the book again.

Nipples On My Knee

Newborn lambs need to be fed every few hours as their systems are quite small, and their requirements and growth are large. They can gain as much as a pound per day, so it does not entail rocket science to figure how much they need to be fed…a few ounces at a time in the beginning, multiple times per day.

The idea of tramping down to the barn every few hours in the winter does not have much appeal. We live in the northeast and most of our lambs come in January to March. Plan B. We made up a corner of the basement with a large plastic sheet to cover the floor. For confinement, we stacked hay bales around the area, creating a nursery about four by six feet. Mixed up a formula per the book, and worked out shifts for around the clock feeding. Worked out quite well, but we never did it again to that extent. We evolved better methods in later years than using the basement. It's similar to having a litter of puppies minus the mother.

Bulldog looked like a lost cause. She could not even lift up her head, would not attempt to eat or drink. Being new to sheep, it became a question of what is it, and what do we do? I felt nothing would be lost by giving her massive doses of the old standby, penicillin. When all else fails, shoot em up. Did not think it could do any harm, as it looked like the battle was already decided. I had to get liquid into her, as she would not drink. This was done several times a day with a very large syringe, minus the needle. After several days' care, and much penicillin, things began to look up. We felt pleased and elated that we were able to bring her back from the other side. We might become sheep vets after all! She eventually made a full recovery and went back on the trailer to the auction. Not knowing what caused the problem in the first place, it seemed the prudent thing to do.

Her lambs continued to thrive, and were really a joy to

have. They were named chop, for the female, and roast for the male. Both grew to adulthood, and chop went on as a member of our flock for many years and roast was sold to a friend and neighbor. He was starting out with a few sheep and needed a ram. It became obvious that if we wished to continue in the sheep and lamb business, we would need a ram, so back to the livestock auction. One evening they ran this large red headed ram into the ring. Now I must admit, I had never seen a red headed and red-legged sheep. I felt the price was fair and I had the need…sold.

Bought our first flock ram by the pound, without knowing anything about him. He could have been old, sick, not able to breed, but luck was with us again. Often dumb luck trumps skill or knowledge.

Thus began our long acquaintance with the Tunis breed of sheep. Tunis sheep have many characteristics, one of which is prominent wrinkles that run across their noses from side to side. Earlier, I mentioned that my wife, Debi, is a bit of a Trekkie, thus Lieutenant Warf became part of the flock. He turned out to be sterling individual. He was generally mild mannered. I admit we did have one or two "talks." Rule number one, you don't ram the Shepherd. This behavior cannot be tolerated both for my safety and the safety of anyone else that may be in the pasture.

One day, he crossed the line and rammed me. Not being familiar with the Marquis of Queensberry rules for fights with sheep, we took to wrestling in the mud. After a prolonged struggle, I threw him down, minding the fact that he outweighed me, and pinned him. I proceeded to grab him by the nose. Closing off his air with my palm across his nostrils quickly took the fight to a TKO. After much yelling and screaming at him, mostly because I was mad, I let him get up.

He had his head down as if to acknowledge defeat, and moved off. From that time on we got along fine. I became the Alpha ram in the flock. The pecking order was established.

During the breeding season, normally August, I frequently went down into the pasture to observe whom he was breaking grass with. Nothing is more relaxing than a warm summer evening walking in the moonlight across a grassy field. When a ewe is coming in season to be bred, the ram will normally stick right beside her, to ward off any other suitors and be there to service her. I would walk through the pasture with Warf at my side, going around to many of the ewes. I'd walk up to one and ask Warf, "How about this one?" He would go over and give her a sniff. If he thought she was ready, he would proposition her by touching her rear leg with an out stretched foreleg, accompanied by a rather loud nasal grunt. If she had an interest in love, she would stand there, normally turning her head back to look at him, as if to say "Okay, let's do it.' Walking away indicated no interest today. We had a good rapport and I was sorry when the time came for him to leave. Being that we couldn't breed him back to his daughters, as inbreeding is a bad practice which can lead to genetic problems it became time to go on a ram hunt again. He was returned to my point of origin, the livestock auction. He may have gone to another farm, but most likely was sold for slaughter.

I have been asked what will happen to them after the auction. Most people think they are going to be eaten but that is relatively unlikely in this area of the country. There is some ethnic market, but it is rather small. Mutton, which is an adult sheep, is not well received in most of the United States. In the southwestern US, most go to Mexico, where mutton is quite acceptable. I understand it makes a great taco. For this area, they are most likely to become pet food. Look at a can and it may say, "Meat and meat by-products." That could be sheep (or whatever meat they can get cheaply).

As I recall, the price was about what I paid for him when purchased. Not bad, as he sired many good lambs, some of which lines are still in our flock today. Think of buying a used car, using it several years, then selling it for what you paid. He is gone, but not forgotten.

Low and behold, at a later auction there appeared to my eyes, another red ram. Bidders up, price was right, sold! I got a really pleasant surprise when I went to the office to pay for my purchase. When I paid, the lady said. "Here's his papers." He was a fully registered Tunis ram having just been purchased for meat prices. If he had been purchased from a breeder, the price could easily have been at least ten times higher. Little did I suspect, he had a "dark" side we would learn later.

ALABAMA

I was eight months pregnant when Graham trucked in five big very pregnant white ewes. He unloaded them into the pasture. "Come on out! We are now really shepherds." I always loved animals and the outdoors. However, I have never owned a pregnant animal, except a gerbil. It doesn't seem my gerbil experience would really count.

I called them my southern ladies. Ladies was used facetiously. These critters would leave hoof prints across your body if you had a can of feed. Each was named accordingly. We had Florida, Virginia, Georgia, Texas and Alabama. Not long after their arrival, as I was returning from the grocery store, I spotted Alabama on her knees stretching her neck under the last strand of wire fencing. The best grass is always on the other side of the fence. The rest of the large body was pushing at the fence. "That ewe will be the first to go down the road!" I said with certainty, my hands on my hips to emphasize the great error this ewe committed. Looking for wandering ewes throughout the neighborhood just wasn't what I expected as a shepherd. Undaunted, Graham began to electrify the fence that weekend.

Our lives continued on as we learned to feed and maintain a healthy flock. Our son was born and the flock took a backseat for a while. Lambing season began, bringing new experiences.

Each ewe did quite well, independent of our machinations. We learned about mastitis and starving lambs. We learned about nature's incredible ability to heal after such close brushes with death. We learned to be mama ewes, since one ewe became so deathly ill.

All the shepherding books direct you toward the philosophy that good ewes produce twins, and triplets are a great event. Our new ewes did twinning! But our surprise of all surprises was Alabama had triplets! "Alabama stays!"

Two more years of lambing pass us by. With each, Alabama easily birthed and nursed triplets. This ewe was incredible! Virginia, Texas and Florida had all been sold. Their bloodlines and Alabama's were now our new flock.

"Alabama's old", Graham said. "She only has four teeth. It's time for her to be sold. She's our best producer, not yet." "Look how bony she is. She doesn't put weight on." I looked at her bones jutting upward through the wool. She was skinny every spring after birthing. She was skinnier than the other ewes, but she always came when I called just to check my hands for some apple slices. "Aw, she's skinny because she gives everything to her lambs."

Well, Graham now knew Alabama's fate was in my hands. I would be the one to decide if she stays or goes every spring. Every spring I felt her bones and waited for her to gain weight after triplets. She was "My Bama." But then came our toughest lambing year. It was a bad year. I cried as our first lamb of the year died before he was born. The ewe had slipped on the ice, wedged herself in an ice crack and struggled until premature birthing began. The lamb basically froze half in and half out of the birth canal. I cried for the ewe who lost the Lamb and I cried for the lamb. I just cried. I was frightened when Graham found Hawaii almost comatose in the sheep shed. Hawaii was one of older ewes. Not quite as old as Bama, but old. Her belly was large with twins. I felt sure those lambs were dead, and sure enough, time proved my gut feeling right. We nursed and treated Hawaii for three days and nights. Unfortunately, we lost Hawaii too.

Hawaii's struggle with life and death forced me to view Alabama differently. If that was, Bama, it would just tear me up. "Alabama gets sold this year," I announced with such authority, Graham said nothing. He knew it had been a real poor season and how Hawaii's death was just to close to being Bama.

We were running scared. We had lost another set of twins when the ewe gave birth in the snow. Why? Why? Was this year so bad?

Bama was large with lambs, her bag almost dragging on the ground. She grunted with each step and gazed at me with eyes of pity. I began to keep her up in the barn at night. My anxiety was rising. One Saturday morning I headed off to the barn. I have the two-way radio in my hand just in case I need Graham's help. My other hand grips a water jug to replenish the water in the barn. The wind whips across the pasture and I am greeted by the flock with various octaves of baa's. I push open the barn door, Right there at my feet is my Bama! She is down! Oh God, she's down! Not my Bama! I call on the radio. "My Bama, my Bama, she's down and she won't get up!" I run to the other side of the barn to put the radio down. As I turn to rush to Bama's side, I see two frightened little lambs hidden amidst the farm implements of rakes and shovels. So she lambed! But she should be up on her feet

I looked Bama over and saw the remains of her birthing. I held her head then tried to coax her to stand. She finally got up and baa-ed a low sickly baa. I picked up her lambs and led

Bama into a stall. "Bama, you sure have given me a scare!" I called up to the house to give them an update. No one had heard my earlier frantic cry, the radio was off up at the house.

I continued my morning tasks in the barn. As I entered the sheep feed area to fill the troughs, there in the corner was this large lamb. Bama's? I checked the other ewes we kept in the barn that night, but none had shown any evidence of birthing. I called up to the house. Gosh darn, Bama did it again! Another set of triplets! After securing this lamb with its mama, I called up to the house. "Gosh darn, Bama did it again! Triplets again!" You should see this last one, it is really big. And large it was. That last lamb weighed in at sixteen pounds. The others were ten and twelve pounds. They were promptly named Blast, Artic and Chill. Bama was not well. Apparently that sixteen-pound lamb ripped her up. She did not want to nurse these lambs. Her usual foghorn baa was now pitifully weak. We doctored her as best we could. We bottle fed her lambs for her. Chill became very weak and joined our family up at the house. He died three days later. Bama is now out with the other ewes. Her baa is back to its old tone and she visits me to check my hand for a treat. Her other two lambs are healthy and visit me to search for a bottle.

Yep, Bama goes this year, I'll miss her.

POPCORN

Debi is watching the three day old twin lambs, but not with the usual enthusiasm. Her eyes watch her son George extol all the wonderful virtues of these lambs to Carole, a neighbor.

"They are twins, Miss Carole, and I help take care of them," George announces. His pride showed in the little puffed out chest and the extra strut as he stoops to stroke a lamb.

"What are their names, George?" Carole asks gently. The chatter between the adult and the child becomes inaudible as Debi's attention draws toward the sounds in the other stall; a heart wrenching grunting and frequent, shallow, difficult breaths. A plaintive "Baa-aaa-aa" vibrates through the barn.

"Oh, God, can I help this ewe? Please, nature, do your thing. Help this ewe birth without my intervention." How much longer can I wait and not lose the lamb, the ewe, or worse yet, both? Debi pleads and struggles within her own thoughts. The scene before her of George, Carole, and the new life is glazed over by the fear and the memories of problem births in the past. It comes back in a torrent of thoughts and images.

Debi didn't grow up a country girl, she was from the suburbs. She had never witnessed births, or for that matter, deaths, until she met Graham. He's the one who brought the sheep into their lives.

Each birthing season brought their share of new lambs cavorting around the pasture, a few orphans to raise, and the problem births.

Fortunately, Graham was home each time to assist a ewe with a problem birth. If George was not in bed for the evening, Debi would help Graham with the birthing. There was that one time…and Debi can still vividly recall death's pungent odor wafting from the womb. Birth and death are so close at times.

Debi frequently held Graham back on interfering in a birth. "Let nature do her thing for a while" she would advise. Now, there is no one to advise Debi. Carole has assisted in birthing cows and hogs, so has some experience. That is some help and comfort. But Debi realizes her actions will probably decide the fate of this ewe and her lamb.

The ewe's bleating is frantic. Hooves are scrambling to right herself. Debi glances over the stall wall. The ewe is upon her feet, bleating in anguish. The ewe's intense labor has been partly successful. The lamb's hoof and either a nose, or another hoof, is showing.

I guess I will need to go in and see what I can do. I don't feel I can wait any longer. Debi slides open the stall door to look directly into the ewe's terrified eyes. The ewe proceeds to race around the jug.

"She won't even let me help her!" Debi's thoughts were screaming as her shoulders drooped under the weight of uncertainty. "I am going to have to catch her and throw her down!" The realization of having to struggle with the ewe causes Debi to question, again, her decision to intervene. Will the lamb and ewe incur additional harm by using brute force? Graham always threw the larger ewes; was Debi capable of getting this ewe down?

The stall door is latched and Debi decides she must catch

and help this ewe. The ewe has the advantage, as she weighs about two hundred pounds. She begins to rapidly navigate the circumference of the jug, avoiding Debi's clumsy attempts at capture. After five good rounds, Debi catches her and struggles to throw her down. Stretching far beneath her, Debi grabs one leg, pulls, and the ewe tumbles down with a resounding thud onto the hay covered floor. Carole quickly enters to restrain the ewe's head, while Debi positions herself to pull on the lamb.

"Push, Dolly, push" is the resounding call in the barn as Debi pulls and wiggles at those little hooves with all her might. The incredible force of labor begins again as the ewe groans and thrashes in pain. But, nothing happens.

"Push, Come on Dolly, push." The ewe grunts and groans. Debi pushes her feet against the ewe's back end and pulls harder. Still, nothing happens.

"Come on Dolly" Debi demands, as she again grips the lamb's hooves and pulls. The ewe groans a long and low whine that rips through the soul. Nothing happens.

My hands keep slipping. I can't get a good grip."

"We use ropes on calves" Carole piped in.

"George, get me some hay string from upstairs, over the lawnmower handles", shouted Debi.

"Okay" shouts George, as he bounds up the hayloft stairs, glad to be of assistance.

Debi continues to try. Her feet are pushing against the ewe, her hands are wrapped around the tiny hooves, and she pulls and wiggles. The ewe arches her head back, eyes wide in terror, and groans in pain. Debi's hands slip off the hooves again. Still nothing happens. Wrap some hay string around the hooves trying to provide some firmer grip.

"Push Dolly, push" Debi says as she rocks and wiggles once again, trying hard to hold her grip. The ewe bleats and rocks her head. Suddenly, the lamb just slips right out, as if petroleum jelly was rubbed all over it. Debi's eyes grow large and round in surprise. Jubilation dances through Debi's heart. A smile the length of the Mississippi broadens across her face. She did it!

The lamb is very large, especially for a first year ewe. Debi starts wiping the lamb with a towel and stops in mid-wipe, the lamb is not breathing!

What Debi recalls she must do sounds so cruel and barbaric. "I need to pick this lamb up by the hind legs and swing it around." The centrifugal force should clear the airways of mucus; force its lungs to work hopefully.

Carole left the jug. Debi picked up the lamb's hind legs, still slippery from birth. Her grip tightens as she begins to swing him around the jug. The lamb's body stretches so far, it appears it will scrape the walls. Debi's heart is stretched out just as far and feels as if it also is scraping the walls.

After the fourth rotation, Debi gently pulls the lamb toward her chest. She cradles it and feels the breath of life, warm, wet and floppy eared. She lays the lamb gently in front of his mother. Feeling triumphant, yet humbled, Debi quietly leaves the jug. The ewe and the lamb need this quiet time for their bonding process. Nature can carry on from this point.

Later, George and Debi go back down to the barn to check on the ewe and the lamb. Debi lies down on the freshly bedded hay floor looking at the lamb. He is white with liver spots, like a Dalmatian. You're the funniest looking lamb in the flock she tells him. "The cutest thing since popcorn" Debi whispers, as she strokes the lamb's warm, wet nose. Thus the inspiration came for his name.

DANCER

Dancer came to us in the usual way. There was nothing unusual about his birth from a crossbred ewe we had named Diamond, or with our Tunis ram. Little could we have ever guessed how much he would add to our lives over the years! At the time he was just another meat lamb, one of many born that year.

Diamond was an attractive red ewe, or Tunis sheep. They are known as "The Red Heads", and possess a strawberry to russet coloration on their faces, ears and legs with wool that varies from white to a cream color. If you can remember the movie "The Ten Commandments", they are being driven across the parted sea by the shepherds. If you look closely, they are Tunis sheep. Different from the Tunis of today, they tended to have more of a chocolate color head. Today's Tunis is a lighter color due to being bred to white sheep years ago, and are more correctly identified as American Tunis.

A piece of trivia: George Washington was a breeder of Tunis sheep. The Tunis breed in the United States, were almost lost due to most of them being eaten during the Civil War. Even today they are considered a minor species in this country but are making a comeback.

Dancer was an unusually large lamb, weighing in at fifteen

pounds at birth. This compares to our normal weights of around ten to eleven pounds. Not that unusual, in itself, as he was a single birth lamb, where twins are the norm. The largest lamb we have had was seventeen pounds, which the ewe couldn't have given birth to without our help. These lambs, we normally refer to as pulls (More on this in a later story, "Lambo"). Dancer was a very active individual, bouncing around in the pen, thus he naturally became known as Dancer. He also was having a hard time keeping his legs under him, as he was stepping in his mother's slippery afterbirth, causing his feet to go out from under him. This made it seem as if he was dancing.

We are always watching, though not normally until several months of age, for potential show entries. His size impressed us. We look for lambs that standout, for showing in the Maryland State sheep and wool festival.

My son, George, took him to train as his project. Training consists of getting the animal accustomed to people, being handled, walking on a lead, standing when you wish him to be quiet, and generally behaving.

Lambs tend to be very standoffish, and at times you would think they are crossbred with squirrels. I guess nature breeds this into them for their survival. They tend to have a natural fear of anything larger than them that isn't covered with wool. He was turning out to be such an easygoing lamb. George also taught him something I had never seen before. He broke him to ride. Both of them were young, my son being six at the time, and a mutual bond formed between them.

It would tickle me silly to come home from work and see my son riding around in the pasture on his lamb. I have always regretted that I did not have the foresight to take some pictures, or video them. It's a kind of thing you can never duplicate.

Dancer never offered any resistance to this. In fact, he may have enjoyed it and it was a sight to see.

I would kid people, being the wag that I am. We had told George that Dancer was a pony. I'm sure he knew better than that, but anytime you can bring people a smile, it is always worth the effort. We also tried, for a time, to use a small pony saddle, but it became quickly evident, the physical anatomy of a lamb is different. Their backs are such that a saddle would not fit. Lambs do not have much in the way of withers like a horse or a pony. There is not a back rise to keep the saddle from sliding off to the side. One just doesn't know something will not work until you try it.

We entered Dancer in the Maryland Sheep and Wool Festival (probably the largest sheep show east of the Mississippi River), into the event known as the carcass contest. We were new to showing, (although we had attended the contest the previous year to watch and learn), and had decided that it was worth a shot. My thought was "We can do this!"

To show the animal in its pure form, a requirement is they are closely shorn within five days of the judging. This entails removing as much of their wool as possible. You try to get a smooth skin, without any nicks or cuts. Envision, in your mind, a bald sheep. You don't need to be a judge to see a thin or overly fat lamb. Even if you don't know sheep or lambs, you recognize poor body conformation. Nothing can hide these things from the eyes of an experienced judge.

The show consists of all the lambs being shown in the ring before a livestock judge, who picks and grades on the structure and conformation of the lambs, based on his years of experience.

The lambs are then loaded on a trailer and taken to a local slaughter house to be rendered. Then, three days later, a USDA inspector checks the carcass and grades them based on a given set of guidelines.

The meat is graded on many parameters, such as chop eye, loin size, fat content and yield grade. In other words, how much, in retail cuts, can be expected from the animal?

The final placing is a combination of the live, and on the hook, carcass grading of the lamb. The results are posted, along with photographs of the meat at the main show the following week. Not to take anything away from the judges, the final result can occasionally vary. The judge cannot see inside the lamb, thus the reason for the hook judging. A lamb may be fatter than desired, or have too small of a chop.

This type of show is very objective, not based on how pretty you have the lamb, how well you sheared, or how cute the handler. George should have won easily, being the youngest and in our slightly biased opinion, the cutest.

Over the years not very many sheep people enter this particular contest. Why put your best animals into a contest where they will not be returned? Might they not be more valuable as potential breeding stock?

In our case, we are only breeding for the meat trade. So the end result, in which the lamb is slaughtered, is not an issue. Over the years, the slaughterhouse, which also runs a butcher store, has always made us an offer for the carcass. They get a no risk chance to pick and choose among the best for their trade. The price offered has always been fair, and saves us having to pay the cost of packing and selling privately. Our main interest is that it gives us exposure, and a non-biased method to evaluate our breeding, feeding and raising operation. If we place well, it tells us we are on track, and doing things correctly. An overly fat lamb tells us cut back somewhat on the grain the next year. Not fat enough? Feed more grain the next year.

Now it may seem strange to be raising sheep for fat, but the meat buying public likes to see some fat on the meat they buy, but not an excessive amount. For contest purposes, a standard thickness target is used. Points are deducted based upon this standard. The biggest lamb does not necessarily win as being too fat is a fault, and causes trimming loss during cutting. As opposed to large impersonal sheep operations, most entrants tend to be smaller operators who can put more time and effort into their animals.

The contest was usually held the week before the main show. This was due to the need to have the hook judging and grading, beforehand. The results and photographs would be displayed in buildings open to the public and would take place on the show grounds in an outdoor covered arena. The same area would be used the following week for the main show judging.

I am using the past tense, as several years later the contest was changed. The general consensus of the people running the event was that more people would enter if they would not lose their animals. Why enter your best stock to be slaughtered?

The current contest is done during the main show so the public can participate and watch the judging. At the end, they are invited into the show area to inspect and feel the lambs first hand. The judge is a computer program. Yep, electronics rule. The judge applies vegetable oil to the lambs back, then goes over the area with an ultrasonic probe connected to a computer. In the way doctors use ultrasound on pregnant women, the screen shows the internal structure of the lamb. Then, based upon the sonic readings, calculates the inside of the lamb. Isn't technology wonderful? I preferred the previous method. Perhaps I am just old fashioned? I do not believe the computer can be nearly as good as an eye. This method has become the standard for analyzing meat animals and has achieved wide acceptance. The main advantage, per the show committee, is you get to take your entry home after the show.

Well, you take them home if you have to, but in our case they are always for sale. For several years we have taken some of our registered Tunis lambs with us, not to show for meat, but to sell. Sometimes it works. Sometimes we bring everyone home.

One year, someone liked one of the lambs I showed for meat, so much, he bought him from me to use as a flock ram. He paid less than he would have for registered stock, but above what he would have brought at the livestock auction. The ones we show for carcass are all crossbred. We crossbreed to get the best lamb we can.

The arena floor is covered with sawdust. Along one side are a series of chain link pens about six feet square with a gate. On the backside of the pens is a series of bleachers from which people can watch the judging. The lambs in the contest are placed in the pens so that anyone can look at them if they have an interest. Mostly, the lookers are other exhibitors sizing up the competition. It is held before the main show and there really isn't any public for this event. Most of the people there are the participants and several dozen people who make up the event committee. Their main interest is finalizing plans for the show which starts the following Friday.

We brought Dancer in, put him into our designated pen, and made sure he had fresh water and was clean. One of the features of the day was lunch. The committee would break for a buffet lunch and we were invited to join in. It's always a good feed and the price is right. We get to ride for free.

My son decided to be an entrepreneur and was sitting up in the bleachers with a small pad and sign offering to draw you a sheep. Well, the committee members were all very busy discussing the last minute plans for the festival, so my son went largely unnoticed. That was a blunder on my part. I should have asked someone to go to my son and give him a quarter to draw them a sheep. I still rue that to this day. I am sure it would have meant a lot to him. And I am quite sure he was very disappointed with the lack of interest.

When the judging is about to start, the lambs are taken by their exhibitors outside behind the arena to be weighed and ear tagged with a large colored tag. They are then posed for pictures, rear, side, and front, with the tag number showing. These pictures are used for identification and shown with the final pictures of the meat. In other words, the before, and the after.

George got several strange looks from the other exhibitors, when he got on his lamb and rode him out back to be weighed. For him, that was always the easiest way to get Dancer from point A to point B. Dancer never objected. I doubt most people had ever seen such a sight, or even considered it to be possible. The only similar thing I can think of is mutton busting. That is an event at some rodeos, in which young children are challenged to ride an adult sheep. It's the children's equivalent to bronco or bull riding. The sheep must think something on their backs is a predator, like a coyote, or mountain lion, and try to get it off. The children all wear helmets, and heavy clothes to give some protection from the usual outcome…the child meets the dirt. Dancer weighed around 100 pounds. My son probably weighed half of that, so Dancer had no problem carrying him.

The animals were called, and the exhibitors line their charges next to each other in the center of the arena. George proudly stood out there holding Dancer by his side, doing the best that can be expected of him for his six years. The judge came by, checked Dancer's general conformation, felt his sides, and judged him on his loin width, length and leg thickness.

I don't remember the exact number, but there were probably about eight lambs. We did not place in the top three. As I recall, we were sixth. At least, we did not finish dead last. We felt good. It was our first showing and felt we could do better in future shows. George would have made any parent proud for his professional effort.

The lambs are then led onto the trailer for their last journey. George led Dancer over and helped load him into the trailer. When he returned he said to me, "I hope Dancer enjoys being slaughtered." It felt as if a cold steel hand reached in and tore my heart out. He wasn't crying, but I could see him being brave beyond his age. I admit I felt tears in my eyes and thinking "What have I done to my son"? In somber silence, we gathered up our water pail, cleaning materials, clippers, and such, and set off for home. I don't think either one of us spoke about what happened on the long drive home.

That evening, Debi and I discussed about how I felt. I had a hurt, inside, and while George didn't say anything, I am sure he felt the same way. How does one correct a big wrong? We decided to try to undo what was done.

I got up at 4:30AM and headed down to the slaughterhouse. All the way there, I played it over in my mind. Will I be too late? Do they kill the night before? Will they give Dancer back? We tend to think the worst and our own minds can be our worst enemy. There was no one there when I arrived. I sat in my truck, playing the whole scenario over and over in my mind. Did I make it in time? Did they kill the previous night when the lambs were brought in? Never having done this before, I was haunted with doubts.

As dawn's light washed over the parking lot and building, I

looked inside the covered building and saw some lambs. Dancer was there! Dancer was alive! Yes! There was hope after all! Eventually, people arrived and I explained the situation to them. They understood and were very sympathetic. They gladly got Dancer and handed him back to me.

The drive back home was light like I was flying. The weight was lifted from my shoulders. I had pulled it off, a victory snatched from the jaws of death. It was a beautiful morning, the sky was cloudless, and the world suddenly seemed righted after being upside down. Arriving back at the house, I was greeted by my wife and my son, and, as I recall, we all had a tear or two. The wrong was now righted. Life was good!

Since our farm is a breeding operation, and we did not consider Dancer breeding stock, I told George he could keep Dancer, but he would need to be castrated. If you've ever had a pet animal neutered, it's nothing like that. A domestic pet would be transported to a veterinarian, which is usually a clean, bright, hospital-like setting. The pet is left there and you come back later to pick it up and take them back home, all nice, neat, and proper. With farm animals it's a little bit different. I have previously bred and raised horses. The veterinarian frequently performs the operation with the stallion standing. But he may also have the horse lie down, depending on what he prefers, but usually outside, and in a grassy area. After he administers an anesthetic, the deed is done.

Dancer's neutering was a bit different. My wife Debi scheduled his visit with our vet, who is also one of very few that will treat sheep. She also has her own flock and is always the court of last resort when we have had problems with which we could not deal, mainly the due to the cost. It can cost the asset value of the sheep just to have her come out to the farm. In the end, economics rule.

Dancer lost his manhood on the tailgate of our pickup truck at the vet's office. And so, it was snip, snip, clip, clip, and it was over. His testes went rolling down the driveway. Oh, the humility of it all! He was then put back in a large dog crate we use for lambs and returned home.

It is a rather simple operation, slightly more involved than usual, as lambs are normally done within a week of birth while their "parts" are quite small. Most shepherds' do their own lambs at birth or shortly thereafter, as it's a rather routine procedure. We have always chosen to "not" do our rams' lambs, as in our opinion, they do better whole. It has never posed any problems for us, so why risk any small possibility of a docking procedure problem. He came through the whole operation in fine shape, but I swear, his baa is a little higher now.

Over the years, I think Dancer has been invited to more events than I have. Well, he does have a cute wooliness about him. One of the nature centers our county has, sponsors an herb and craft festival each year. The people in both our county nature centers know us, and we were invited to attend. For his part, Debi made our son, George, a costume that resembled a medieval serf. He spent the day in costume, wandering around the event with his sheep on a lead. To help with his entrepreneurship, dancer was fitted with a set of horse saddlebags. They had a sign on his side, which read, "Dancers wool, $0.25." The Baggies contained a handful of Dancers raw wool from his last shearing. Whether it was the appeal of the wool or for the same reason adults will patronize a child's lemonade stand, the wool sold well, and George made a small amount of money for his effort.

I remember clearly the next year when we came back. Several people were overheard, exclaiming, "Here comes

Dancer!" He really is a pleasure to work with, and we will sorely miss him when he goes. He's like family.

On another occasion, we were asked to bring Dancer, along, to an Arts and Crafts festival. It was quite a distance away, in another county, so the lady requesting the visit offered to pay us for the day. The small payment we agreed upon was to cover the cost of our trip (not that we would make a profit from the endeavor).

We arrived at the affair, which was held on the grounds of what was an old estate. The craft people had set their tables around a grass field about two hundred feet in diameter and we had an assigned location along the path just before the circle. We shared the area with another person who had brought one of their llamas.

The weather was pleasant, the temperature mild, everything was good, save the timing. As I recall, it was one of those days where there were many different events scheduled, so it became clearly evident, attendance was lacking. We had arranged to be able to use one of the buildings for a source of electric to be able to power a computer printer. We had tried this before, with very limited success. The idea was to take pictures with a digital camera of people, and children, with Dancer and sell the photos. The children were seated on the back of a large sheep, normally, with a large smile, which has an appeal to most parents. We also kept some feed handy for those brave enough to allow Dancer to eat from their hands, after we explained that sheep do not eat meat. They will lick the grain from a child's open palm (or palms, if the children are very small). Well, by mid-afternoon, it became painfully evident that the day was going to be a bust. I believe more exhibitors showed up than visitors. It was kind of sad, as I believe people had probably paid a fee to attend and set up a table. I suspect most vendors would have been lucky to sell enough to pay the fee, much less produce a profit.

Becoming quite bored, I decided to walk around and explore the various tables and vendors. Dancer accompanied me on the rounds. Now keep in mind, he heels like a dog, and stays right by my side as I walk. I would walk up to a table that caught my interest and hold my hand down, palm back, in front of him and say, "stop!" He would seem to stop on command and stand quietly by my side. When I finished looking, I would wave my palm in front of him and say, "walk!" and as if by command, he would walk off with me. Everyone thought we had a trained animal that responded to voice commands. It really has nothing to do with either the hand commands or verbal words. It has to be the showman in me. This is not something we have really ever trained him to do, and perhaps was a leftover from when my son trained him to be shown. It does leave an impression on people, though.

Now, due to his color and size, he does not fit into most people's impression of a sheep. He wasn't small, white, and wooly. He has matured to about the size of your average Saint Bernard dog. Once again, my ornery nature rose to the fore. If I were asked what he was, my usual response was, "He's a rare breed of dog called a Himalayan wooly." I believe many people actually bought this explanation. I never said I was a very serious person!

The end of the day came, and we packed up our printer and laptop, never having had any photograph customers. I doubt that we even had more than a dozen or more people come by. I dropped the tailgate and Dancer jumped in for the ride home. You have to love an animal, regardless of what kind it is, for having an easygoing, pleasant nature. He was just a natural born showman.

Another regular outing Dancer goes on is the Easter Bunny trains at the local tourist railroad. I've been associated with them in one capacity or another for more than the last ten years. I've worked on the train, sometimes as an engineer, or any other position. We are all volunteers. They asked if we could do a small petting zoo to complement the bunny trains at Easter.

The zoo has varied over the years depending upon what we have at the time. Perhaps we would bring a rabbit, or a chicken, or a lamb. Of course we would also bring Dancer. We would set up on the grass behind the station using the rack from the truck turned upside down. The rack is used for any lamb we bring, usually a bottle lamb, as they are accustomed to people and being handled. Another staple is a thermos bottle of warm lamb milk and a small bag of sheep food. Children love to either feed them, or give the lamb a bottle.

One of the things I have always loved to do is ask the ladies to put their fingers deep down in his wool and wiggle them around. When they take them out, they usually remark how soft their hands are. Gleefully, I explain that they have just received a "skin treatment", as the lanolin on their hands is the same thing used in most skin treatments. I ask them to feel how soft my hands are, being in the sixty-year-old range, due to years of handling sheep. It kind of rubs off and isn't anything special I did. If you want soft hands, get a sheep!

Dancer is always easy, as he just stays with us. One time I walked up the ramp to where you go to enter the train. He stayed by my side and the children looking out all thought he was coming on board. That caused quite a few smiles and titters from the kids. I am sure they would have loved it. But sheep do not house break, and I choose not to chance an accident. I have no doubt he would have followed me in without hesitation. It has always been well received, and the only problem we have is taking a bathroom break. The facilities are across a busy street that runs beside the station. If one of us needs to use them, when we leave to go, Dancer takes that as his cue to follow. It must look strange to people when we have to hold our hands over Dancer's eyes so he can't see the person leave. I truly believe that he enjoys his outings as a chance to get away from the farm and see different things. Besides, he's a "people" sheep.

Last week was foot-trimming day. Sheep, as well as horses and other livestock, need periodic pedicures. Debi was doing the trimming while I handled the worming. We frequently double team to finish the needed work faster. She would throw the animal and stand it on its butt in front of her. Take the legs one at a time and trim the hooves. Dancer would come over to help. Now, he is sweet and lovable, but makes it hard to work with his nose almost in your face. He really was not trying to get in the way, just looking for attention. If you took a minute and gave him a chest rub, he was happy as a clam. He puts his nose in the air and you would swear his eyes roll back in his head.

After somewhere around eleven years, or so, Dancer became quite arthritic and started to have trouble getting around. We knew it was time for him to be humanely put to rest. I am sure anyone who has had to have a pet put down can relate to this. It's a heart wrenching time, but we felt it must be.

FROSTY

We had an overnight snowstorm that dumped about a foot of snow on us. To make it easier on the sheep and lambs, it is our standard practice to go down to the pasture and plow a path from the barn to the stream to make it easier on the stock to get to fresh water. I had just plowed back from the stream to behind the run-in shed when I discovered something that angered me. There, behind the barn, I could see lambs lying in the snow, quite dead and frozen.

Jumping down from the tractor, I found, to my dismay, three lambs on top of the new snow. Two were quite dead and frozen, but one, covered with ice, still had a spark of life. Her wool was crusted with ice and snow, but she still had that spark. Quickly, I took her into the warmth to submerge her in tepid water to thaw out slowly. The spark grew brighter, and she started to come around. After she warmed to what we felt was an acceptable level and was dried off, she was returned to the care of her mother in the barn.

It was only through luck that I had gone down to plow when I did. Surely, if it had been later, we would have lost her, too.

She was an interesting looking lamb with a mottled white face with black splotches. She had pendulant ears that hung down, making her look more like a goat than a sheep.

Happy to say, this one ended on a happy note. The name came naturally. She became Frosty, the snow lamb, or just "Frosty." As I am writing this book, she is still here as a valued member of the flock at the ripe old age of six.

DOZEN

Anyone who has many animals knows that there comes along the "certain" one that stands out in your mind. Whether it is a good or a bad thing is always up to conjecture. On our farm, we had "Dozen." Where she came from is anyone's guess. The only thing I know for sure is how our paths crossed.

Every year there are many shows held around the state. The ones I am closest to are the 4H fairs. 4H is a great group of children who vie with their animals to be the best of the show. Most, if not all their entries are raised with pride and loving care, and possibly spoiled rotten. You only have to attend a show to watch how lovingly they act and the great care given to each, whether it is a cow, a rabbit, or other animal.

After the shows are over, many of the show animals are offered up for auction with the proceeds often to be saved for their future education. Many businesses and companies purchase the animals, to show support for the children and 4H. The prices paid are usually many times the normal market value. Supermarkets often buy and use the purchase in their advertisements.

Due to the large amount of types shown, there are always some that need to be sold after the show. This is due to lack of space, or as some do not live on farms and may have been kept at another location. Or perhaps, just for closure.

In the town I live in, which still maintains some rural characteristics, there is a livestock auction. Want to buy a cow? Sell a sheep? This is the place. I've seen llamas, ostriches, and all kinds of creatures come through the sale ring.

Being a breeder for the lamb market, and not really caring about the pedigree of the sheep, or its papers, I have found it to be a great place to pick up quality breeding stock. Now if you were to just pick at random, you have a good chance of buying someone's problems. I can say this from experience, having been burnt several times in the past. It does go either way; they could be fine animals that are offered for sale for other than health reasons. Perhaps they are going out of the business and have a need to reduce head count. Think of buying an animal at auction like buying a used car. You can go down in the pens, and "kick the tires." You check what you can but keep in mind, all sales are final. It is always buyer beware. I've purchased two flock rams, and mostly through dumb luck, got good ones.

It is easy to spot 4H animals, by their distinctive ear tags. I watch for a "few good ewes." The large orange ear tags all have 4H imprinted and their 4H number. This was how Dozen entered into my life.

That day at the auction I purchased three ewe lambs to add to my flock. I feel safer buying former 4H animals, knowing the care and attention they have had lavished upon them by their owners. Chances are good that they've gotten the best of care and feeding. Plus, they will be quite accustomed to people and being handled. The real reason is that I am a rather frugal Scot who likes to buy on the cheap. At the auction animals are sold for meat value by the pound.

Being that we have always named our sheep, one became Clover, after the 4H juniors, the other two had large paint brands on their backs. One had a large number seven, so she became Lucky. And as you have probably guessed by now, the third ewe had a large number twelve branded on her. Hence, the name, Dozen.

Dozen looks like a pure-bred Suffolk ewe. She has the characteristic jet-black head with no wool, and black legs. She may be a purebred, but in our operation, it matters little to us. Produce matters, not papers. If I ever really want to trace her back, I can probably do so through 4H.

As she matured, it became obvious to all of us that she was pushy, had no regard for personal space, or human life and limb. Now, sheep are not the smartest limb on the animal tree, but in many ways she is smart. She learned early on that if she pushes on a door that is not securely latched, it opens. The only one that we have that requires latching doors, behind us, is when we go into or out of the barn. She is the leader of the pack, always being first into any feed or hay.

Now, I must come clean. She has become my pet. I am inclined to overlook her behavior. But I will admit, at times, she stretches even my patience. When I go down to the pasture, there will always be one sheep leading the flock towards me and bellowing like a wounded bull. She walks beside me and escorts me to the barn door, not wanting to miss out on anything to eat. Her nose will always be at the gap where the doors open, trying to push her way in. She has the attitude and manners of a junkyard dog. My wife has even gone to the extent of nicknaming her the "ghetto ewe." As long as she stays on my good side and produces, she stays.

There are times when we pause to reflect that there are things that are beyond our understanding of nature.

The other day, as I went down to the barn to feed, I passed my son on the way back up. I informed him that Debi and I had discussed the physical condition of dozen and felt that she was thinner than we felt she should be. Being in the last weeks of pregnancy, she should be getting some extra feed.

I fed the rest of the flock in the barn, put hay out on the hill, and went back inside to clean up and tend the other ewes with lambs. There came a knock at the door and when I went to see, it was Dozen. It seems strange because I had just mentioned that she should be getting extra feed.

The thought crossed my mind that maybe she can read minds? No, surely not! It must have just been a coincidence. But then again, life is full of mysteries. I'm sure we have all had the experience with an animal where they "seemed" to read our mind. Then again, she does seem smarter than the average sheep.

Now why would we keep such a rude animal? The main reason, Shepherd's pet aside, she has given us two sets of triplets. As I write this story, she is in the process of raising all three without any assistance or continued supplementing. The lambs all have a good rate of gain, and I would love to have all my ewes be like this one, but without the attitude. Several of her daughters have now become breeding members of our flock.

Dozen's first attempt at motherhood was a failure. She gave birth to a sac lamb which was dead when I found it. I wasn't there when she gave birth so the lamb was lost. We are always crestfallen when we loose one, and this got to me, as she was already becoming a pet. Sac lambs can be saved either by the mother breaking the sac at birth, or the Shepherd doing it. It is not a normal delivery, as the birth sac will usually break, before, or during delivery. For us to do it, we must be there when the lamb comes out. Her first year was down the drain.

On her next try things went much better. She gave birth to triplets; two rams and one ewe. For some unexplained reason, she decided the ewe lamb was not hers and rejected it. Nothing we did could convince her that the lamb was hers. For the safety of the lamb, we had to remove her to the house and

feed her around the clock. On the plus side, ewe's fit very nicely in pampers. Just snip a small hole in the bottom for the tail, and you have a solution that allows the lamb free movement around the house. The name came naturally; Orphan Annie.

Annie quickly adapted to life in the house. It was like having a new puppy or kitten. She developed a routine where sleep was the order of the day. When she got hungry, she would seek us out, baaing loudly. We would heat up her bottle, feed her till she was satisfied, and she would usually curl up in the living room in front of the TV. Perhaps she was waiting for animal planet or some similar show to come on.

At about two in the afternoon the sun would come in the front window and shine on a spot by my chair. This became her favorite spot. She would move over to bask and sleep. They grow fast and the need for around the clock feeding only lasts a week or so. She was cute, and a delight to have around, but quickly outgrew the coverage afforded by a diaper. It was time to move her down to the barn. Being older now, she could take more at each feeding, and require them less frequently. She kept complaining that a mistake was being made, she was really a house lamb, but to no avail. The barn was her new home. She has grown up to look like her mother, minus the attitude.

MISS PIGGY

While it doesn't sound like a very flattering name for a lamb, the reason will become clearer as the saga unfolds.

It is the norm, and desirable, for most ewes to have twins. The ewes that have a single birth are rather looked down on, by me, as numbers make the bottom line. I will often chide the ewe who only gives me one with the admonition she needs to try harder, or "get on the truck."

Sometimes it works too well. This year, Tiki took the message to heart and decided to really please the Shepard and have triplets. Now sheep, unlike cows, only have two teats. Cows have four, and normally have one calf. Go figure nature out. Due to the lack of accommodations at the buffet, she decided that one had to go. They make it very clear. No matter how hard the lamb tries, she will butt it and push it away.

This is sometimes the case where several lamb together and the lambs get mixed up. No amount of convincing would make her relent and accept the lamb. If we do not intercede quickly, within hours, the lamb will die.

Being three were taking up the space normally filled with two, all three were lightweights. They only weighed around seven pounds each, where normal weight is around eleven pounds.

This was the third case of rejection we had this year. The first was easy. The ewe only had a single and was kept up in a jug for several days. She was restrained in a halter so her movements were restricted to getting to her hay and water. After three days, she would let the lamb nurse, and was put out. I had named her little ram Tenacious, because no matter how hard she tried to reject him, he would not take no for an answer. He finally won out, and life was good.

The second case was one of my pure bred Tunis ewes. She had twins in the jug, and for whatever reason goes through their one cell brains, decided one of them was not hers. Again the same method was applied. Confinement and restriction was applied.

Several times a day I would go down to the barn, restrain her against the wall, and allow the lamb to nurse off her. This is a normal, tried and proven method with a high success rate.

I would also take a bottle of lamb milk formula to make sure the lamb was receiving sufficient nourishment. This is an around the clock routine, day and night. It's easy to understand why orphans and rejects are a problem to shepherds. It only works well if you have young children who think, "It's neat!" Well, for the first time for us, the method failed. I also tried putting Vicks on the ewe's nose to block her sense of smell, which they use to determine if it is her lamb. Nothing I tried would cause her to accept her little ewe back. I tried to explain to her every day that it really was her lamb, but no dice. It wound up being a frustrating four-week ordeal until the lamb was eating sheep feed and hay, and was able to be on her own. With Tiki's lamb, Miss Piggy, we tried something different this year. Our methods are constantly evolving, year after year.

In the garage I have a large sheet of steel on the floor I use to weld on. I covered it with sheets of cardboard, then straw.

Over the top of it, I placed the upside down rack for the truck and made a pen of about four by six feet. The steel made the floor "moisture" proof. Having her in the garage made the around the clock feedings, easier. I would go out to feed her in a bath robe, overnight.

The "Miss Piggy" name came from my son, due to her constant baaing to be fed. My joke was she needed a fifty-five-gallon drum with a hose and a nipple to keep her satisfied.

After about four weeks, and showing me she was eating sheep feed and hay, it became time for her to join the flock. I would take her out with me to feed and associate with the other lambs. She did not seem to relate to them. I think they begin to believe they are more "people" than sheep. In time I would sneak out of the pasture, when she wasn't looking, and leave her there. If she saw me leave, she would chase after me. She is now integrated with the others and content with her lot.

When I go up to feed the sheep and lambs in the upper pasture, she is right there by my side. At least she has learned to keep out from under foot or run in front of my legs to trip me. She's the only one allowed to come into the feed and hay room with me. Spoiled rotten comes to mind. She has become quite the petting lamb. They normally are very hand shy about being touched, and bolt away. She's definitely the top candidate for the lamb petting zoo.

We had taken a trip, this summer, and had met this zany young lady on the tour bus. When we went to our local bank, we found that she worked there as a customer representative. When my wife went into the bank one day, she asked her to have me bring a lamb to the bank on Friday. Now to my way of thinking, if she was crazy enough to ask, I was crazy enough to do it.

Come Friday, I put a wire dog crate in the back of my

pickup, loaded Miss Piggy, and drove to the bank parking lot. I had just pulled into a parking space when someone pulled up behind me. The gentleman asked if she was for sale. He wanted to get her as a pet for his grandchildren. I gave him a business card and explained he can come out to the farm and we can discuss it. Raised by themselves, they can make quite a nice pet.

Being the wag that I am, I went into the bank, sans Miss Piggy. I had put a small stuffed lamb in my coat. When I went up to her desk, I pulled it out, and said. "You did ask for me to bring a lamb, didn't you?"

She had a customer at the time, and replied, "No, I meant a live one."

I replied, oh, she's out in my truck. At which time, she shut off her computer and her and her customer came out to the parking lot to look. I think at least half the bank employees, at one time or another must have come out to look and pet. Everyone coming in or out of the bank did so, too.

I had explained it is rather impossible to house break a lamb, so prudence dictated I not bring her inside. I had done that once before at the feed store and she embarrassed me by promptly relieving herself on their floor. I asked, and was directed to the paper towels. She learned quickly to ride on the front seat of my pickup truck with a bath towel under her, keeping out of my way, and occasionally, getting up to look out the window.

Her next big outing was the yearly petting zoo I do for the tourist railroad's Easter bunny trains. At the tender age of eight weeks, she is showing me lots of promise as a pet. She and Dancer were as much the stars of the day as the Easter bunny and the train. I would keep her in the pen until the train left or when it came back. With hundreds of small children running around, I was sure she would go into overload. Dancer was his usual laidback self, allowing several dozen children to have their picture taken, sitting on his back. Neither of them needed to be restrained between trains, as there was plenty of nice green grass to munch on, so they stayed put. Both also thrilled many young children, and a few adults, as I always bring some sheep feed for hand feeding. Some parents needed to be assured that sheep do not eat meat or bite, so little hands presented palm up with feed would only be licked, not bitten. Several also had to be assured that Dancer would not "Kick" if the children walked behind him. It turned out to be a hit with the people, although rather tiring, as I had to be in constant attendance. Fortunately, the weather was great.

At the end of the event, I loaded them up and packed my wet naps, water jug, dishes, paper towels, and old towels to head back to the farm. When I got back, I backed up to the grass bank next to the driveway, opened the tailgate, and they unloaded themselves. We walked up the hill, I opened the pasture gate, and they put themselves away. It would be hard to believe you could ask for nicer, easy to manage animals than them. I wonder if she knows that she has a free pass and need not worry about getting on the truck come market day.

As it came to pass, I had a gentleman contact me about buying two lambs for him to raise, for meat. He had goats, but never had any experience with sheep. He came out with his young daughter one afternoon, and the only one she liked was, you guessed it, Miss Piggy. He had decided to try to raise sheep too, so he wanted a ewe and a ram. I was really torn over it, but had to remind myself, either sentimental, or in business. Later, I thought I should have asked for "Visitation rights." Maybe I'll ask, next year.

THE SAGA OF GRATEFUL

The day started like all days, with a trip down to the barn to check and feed.

When I approached the one run-in, I could see a body. Shucks, a dead lamb. That assumption was because there were not any ewes near it. But when I went closer, it moved its head. I entered and saw a lamb, flat on its belly with its four legs all out to the side, like the points of a compass, looking like road kill. When I picked it up, I found it was unable to use its legs. They hung like cooked spaghetti. My mind shifted into shepherd mode. Was it white muscle disease? Perhaps it was spinal damage during delivery?

I found the mother. At least I believe it was, as no other ewe looked to have lambed. She was in another area with a newborn lamb. I took the ewe into a jug in the barn and called my son for assistance. He came down and while I held the ewe, he held the lamb up to the teat so it could nurse. Some of you probably have done this, assuming you raise animals, and it can be quite frustrating. Often, it takes time for the animal to figure out what to do. It helps if you open the lamb's mouth with a finger, and insert teat. Then keep the lamb on. We repeated this process several times a day the first day. I would hold the ewe still while he would hold the lamb to assist it to nurse.

What we have done, previously, was to practice physical therapy with the lamb's legs. Working the legs causes resistance from the muscles. They seem to work, as resistance was felt. We continue the process with the lamb. At the end of the second day, it was able to stand, shakily. It was sort of like looking like at sawhorse. It was able to nurse after we got it up. By the third day, the lamb was stronger and able to get on its feet, with effort. We still restrained the ewe to make it as easy as possible on the lamb to nurse.

Well, just when you feel the battle is going your way, a problem. Seems the ewe is rejecting the lamb. Still being shaky, she knocks it off its feet with her head when it tries to nurse. We continue to restrain the ewe so the lamb can nurse several times a day.

All in all, I guess it's a good thing, as it caused the lamb to get up on its feet constantly and work its legs.

Most sheep people know rejection is rare, but it happens. The ewe checks the lambs butt to verify it is hers. Her milk imprints on the manure. Not so in this case. The lamb is white, and its sister is a normal Tunis red. The ewe rejects it on color and never checks the scent. Being that she goes by color, not scent, it throws out all the usual methods for grafting. Do we continue to restrain the ewe? Should we dye the lamb red? After eight days, we are still restraining the ewe so that Grateful can nurse. It poses an issue with which we all have to deal. What the heck do I do now?

The most practical solution will be to have, and to shutter, another bottle lamb to raise. Not having young children who see this as fun, leaves it to me.

Will prepare one side of the garage again, with the steel sheet on the floor, covered with straw, and my up-turned sheep rack from my truck. It makes a nice nursery and is definitely more convenient than traipsing down to the barn many times a day and night. It also allows more frequent feedings.

I can remember doing it in other years, feeding in the middle of the night in my bathrobe.

And now as Paul Harvey would have said, the rest of the story. Her name came naturally, "Grateful." I kept reminding the lamb to be grateful, for if not for me, she would be dead.

Grateful has progressed beautifully. She only has a few issues. She has become spoiled by being bottle fed. This is normal for bottle lambs, and she takes it to extreme. I offer fine sifted sheep feed, but she declines my offering. At the age of six weeks, she started to nibble on the feed. And I always provide the nicest, leafy, grassy hay I can find.

The real issue is water. She refuses to drink from a container, and only wants to nurse from a bottle, or lamb bar I purchased for her. Its a quart plastic container, like a jar, with a large rubber nipple at the base. I've started to replace the formula with more and more tap water to transition her to becoming a sheep.

Much of a lamb's education comes from copying their mother. They see her eat some grain and they will try it when they are as young as two or three days old. Mom drinks from the stream and they learn this, too. She also has the freedom of being out of the enclosure during the day, thus allowing her to start to graze on the front lawn and greet everyone who comes by. She loves the attention.

When she is out, she tags along with me wherever I go. This includes what I refer to as the lamb step. She will run in front of me to provide a tripping obstacle, hence, the lamb step. As they get a little older they learn, better, how to keep from being under foot. Being that she follows me, I get her to go down to the barn with me to feed the rest of the flock.

I've invited her into the lamb run in an area where I provide free access for the lambs to come into the barn and eat when they are hungry. I can close access to this from inside the barn, and while she was busy eating, quietly close the gate and leave the barn. You never really know if it will work till you try it, but she did not figure it out.

I was concerned she would try to come back up to the house through the fence. My concern was the high voltage on it. The rest of the flock are quite electric fence broke and have learned to keep clear, as it is quite shocking.

Now at the tender age of eight weeks, she has transitioned from lamb to sheep. She still runs to greet me but I guess she has accepted her position as a flock animal and has lots of playmates to keep her occupied and they play and run around together.

I would love to get her a job in a petting zoo, as she would be great at that.

And I will consider spending some time with her to teach her to heal and walk on a leash.

The saga of ewe and me continues…

SPARK, THE LAMB

We had my son and his girlfriend over for Christmas dinner. When she learned that we had day old lambs in the barn, she wanted to see them.

As it turned out, she never made it down, which was just as well. When I went into the stall, I saw a dead lamb on the floor. Closer examination showed the lambs mouth to be cold as ice. It couldn't move or lift its head, but a tiny spark still burned within. I grabbed the lamb and dashed up to the house and went inside with the lamb. I laid the lamb out on a feed bag on the kitchen counter. All shepherds do that, don't they?

I hurriedly started rooting through cabinets trying to locate my tube feeding equipment. Great, I found the tube and hose, but no plunger. Improvise time. By now I was a wild man, as I knew my time was getting short. I located the lamb milk replacer in the bedroom closet where everyone must keep their supply. I made up a mixture of warm lamb milk replacer, cod liver oil, and colostrum.

The part I fear most is inserting the tube down the throat into the stomach. You don't want to do it, but the alternative is death. It is so easy to insert the tube into the lungs, instead of the stomach. I did that once and I am sure you can figure out the result. I put several cc into her, laid her on a towel, and put her on a heating pad in a box. I covered her up, and then had to leave for a dinner engagement. I felt I had done as much as I could and now it was up to her. When we returned about four hours later, we were greeted by a lamb scampering up and down the hallway.

That kind of event makes you want to shout, jump up in the air, and pump your fists in the air. I won! She went from almost dead to quite alive in four hours.

Now, I have a house/garage lamb to raise for several weeks until she is old enough for all solid food. Its only fun if you have young children who think it is neat to do. I am 74 and have been involved with sheep for 25 years. The fun part wore off years ago, but I still enjoy it. She has become the shepherd's pet. I think she knows she doesn't have to fear the truck and has a position for life. The strange part, I guess, is her being a bottle lamb, and now she doesn't know she's a sheep. She doesn't wish to associate with the rest of the flock and seems scared to death of them. I need to feed her separately and away from the rest. She follows me around as long as I am in the pasture.

I guess, being that I hand raised her, she thinks of me as the mommy ewe. Can you say "spoiled rotten", boys and girls? I'll bet you can!

A TYPICAL DAY ON THE FARM

Well, just to give you an example of, we hope, not a typical day, we have learned to accept the way things are. You roll with the punches.

The first order for the day is look out the front window of the house and see if you can get a head count. The lower pasture is visible from the front of our house, save the area behind our small barn and the pole building run in shed, built originally for our horses. After we get the correct count, usually 24-30 its coffee time. If the count comes up short, as it frequently does, the coffee must wait. The second order of the day is going down to the barn and checking everything. As I was making my tour, I found a dead lamb in the run-in we call the solarium. So named, as the side facing the house is green fiberglass panels left over from the barn roof.

The lamb, we call Blue, had been in a struggle for the last several weeks. He was one of the first born for the year and was the largest of triplets. This in itself should have given him the best chance for survival. Despite our best efforts, we were not able to diagnose what his problem was. No matter what we tried, he still was slipping downhill.

Nipples On My Knee

Triplets can be both a blessing and a curse when you are in the lamb business. They often require additional supplementation, and work. This is the kind of thing that starts every shepherd's day, badly, finding a dead animal. Finding a ewe with healthy, on their feet, new lambs helps to balance the scale in the other direction, and re-direct your focus off the death.

When I entered into the barn to check how the other four ewes were doing, I found dozen's smallest triplet, a little ewe, lying there very still.

Now you have to understand the normal behavior of your animals. Young lambs tend to be quite skittish and very active. When I touched her, she barely stirred. Never a good sign.

I moved the mother ewe, Dozen, our farm's bad girl, across the aisle to a clean jug. The lamb stayed behind, which is another warning sign. I called my wife on the intercom and asked her to please bring down a bottle of warm milk replacer, for it is often the case with triplets, the smallest gets short shrift. When my wife, bless her patience, arrived, and after consulting with her, we decided to take the lamb up to the house.

This in itself has become an unfortunate event, which is both good and bad. The good is we normally can save them. The bad is extra work for the family.

My wife made up the special formula of milk replacer, egg, cod liver oil, and sugar. We were able to get some into the lamb using a baby bottle. Not to be confused with bottle babies in petting zoos, they usually do not take to this abnormal manor of feeding. The procedure is to pry their mouth open gently with a finger, have the head elevated slightly, and insert the nipple.

Usually results with a fight and the Shepherd having as much formula on them as gets into the lamb. With luck and heaps of patience, the lamb will learn to suck from the rubber nipple. This greatly aids with the supplementation, which needs to be done several times a day. After they become accustomed to the routine, it gets easier. If it becomes necessary for the supplementing to continue for several weeks, the lambs will almost attack you when they see the bottle. We tell people (and children in particular) to hold the bottle tight, as they will tear the bottle out of your hands in a feeding frenzy. However, it is a rewarding sign that we have won. But as Yogi Berra once said, "It ain't over till it's over."

She was given a place near a hot air register and wrapped in a bath towel. Well, that didn't suit her. Not fond of being left alone, or more than five feet from someone, she would not stay put. If I walked into the kitchen, she would sprint to follow.

Now, tile floors are not compatible with newborn lambs. She would hit the tile and do a split. I wasn't able to get her feet beneath her. Perhaps funny, but I wouldn't allow this to happen again because we don't want her to come to any harm.

She did find her spot in life across my lap in the living room. Now mind you, it is a real joy with this cute trusting life in your lap, but it does cut down your ability to get much done. I was able to get some things accomplished as I have my laptop computer next to my lazy boy recliner. I could sit back and check my E-mail. If someone were to drop by, they might think it's somewhat weird to see a grizzled and bearded old man sitting in the living room with a computer and a lamb, in his lap. The truth be known, there must be some plusses to this business, and those plusses help to offset some of the negatives. If it didn't bring a smile to your face to stroke her as she sleeps in your lap, you must not have feelings for animals. These little lambs are so pure and innocent, not even able to realize that we are trying our best to preserve their lives.

We have had several house lambs in the past so the precedent is well established. One that comes to mind is orphan Annie. Annie was the smallest triplet from Dozen (who seems to weave through this book like a bad dream).

Who can ever understand what goes through that one brain cell mind of theirs? Dozen decided that Annie was not her lamb.

If a ewe thinks that a lamb is not hers, she makes it very plain, very quickly. They will butt and push the lamb away. While it can be quite violent, the lamb needs to be quickly removed for its safety, lest it become injured or killed. It makes you sad to see this. Here is this new life trying to do what nature instilled into its' genes, trying to live, and having a mother who rejects it.

The poor lamb always looks so hopeless and confused as to why this is happening. To tell the truth, we also wonder. Did we handle the lamb after holding another lamb, and did that confuse the mother? Is it natural selection, as it seems to usually be the smallest lamb? We will probably never know. I have asked the ewes, "What is the problem?" But they just reply, "Baa."

There are methods to treat this that vary by shepherd. The usual method is to humanely restrain the ewe, within reach of food and water, but unable to turn around to stop the lambs from nursing. Often a stand is made, or bought, that resembles a cow stanchion used for milking. The ewe's neck is held on both sides so that she cannot turn around. That may seem mean. But it is for a short duration and no harm is done to the animal. Once the lambs have nursed for several days, the ewe's milk imprints on the lamb's manure, which is the scent the ewe goes by to determine her own lambs.

Yes, she smells their butts to determine if they are hers. She will do this constantly to make sure that only her lambs are feeding from her. If she is not satisfied with the scent, she will butt and push the lamb away.

In the past I have relied on an old trick from my horse breeding days.

And you thought Vicks was only good for chest congestion. I rub Vicks on their nose. It has the effect of dulling their sense of smell. It's a favorite, I've learned, of transporters moving stallions in a van with mares. Sometimes, this is all that is needed.

We have also restrained a ewe that lost her lambs to graft either an orphan or rejected lamb on her. This works well for us as bottle lambs, while a pleasure, are also a lot of additional work. If all goes well, the ewe will accept the new lamb as her own.

Now I'm sure any sheep people reading this will either be shaking their head either in the affirmative or disbelief, but as I have said before, "One must do whatever is needed to be done…and works." Everyone has their own methods, and I won't say what is right or wrong. It's the final results that count, at the wire.

After I needed to finally arise, for reasons you can suspect, I went around and selected an appropriate size cardboard box. I lined it with a bath towel and gently placed her in it. No way! She jumped up and knocked the box over, then scampered up to me. On the second try, I selected a higher box.

She started baaing for all she was worth because she could not see anyone.

I brought her and the box into the living room so she could see me and I could work on my laptop. After she got quiet, I put a towel over the top of the box to cover it and simulate nighttime. She went to sleep.

After two feedings she seemed much better. Debi took her back down to the barn to her mother. She watched her nurse, so she left her, and came back up to the house. Thankfully, she was accepted back into the fold. I arrived back from picking up sheep feed and went down for the afternoon feeding.

Another of our ewes, Gremlin, has been off since she lambed. A sheep that does not eat is always a warning of problems. Her single lamb seems normal in attitude and action. Her nursing, or lack of nursing, was not an issue. Were she not nursing, the lamb would be dead. So, it was time for a conference. We do a lot of this. Perhaps, you could call it sheep-raising by family conference. Three minds are always better than one.

Many issues are discussed among the family and various avenues are considered. We retired back up to the house to consult our sheep manuals. When in doubt, read the "instructions."

Now books can be a real aid, especially if you don't know all the answers. And then, even after reading the book, much comes down to common sense.

The books can never replace real life experience. We each took a book to review symptoms and discuss probable causes and treatments. The challenging part is you can't ask the patient any questions or ask them how or where they hurt. This is why we need and admire veterinarians.

We had shot her full of penicillin the previous day, checked her for milking, took her temperature, checked her udder, and smelled her breath. Smelling their breath is looking for a sign of an ailment known as ketosis. At least that is what the book implies. Yep, she acted sick!

I won't go into a detailed medical explanation as I am not trying to write a vet manual or a guide to raising sheep. It's just an attempt to get a smile about my life with EWE.

Nothing came up to point in a specific direction.

You learn that any effort is better than none. Our consensus was milk fever.

While we don't always get it right, even doctors sometimes miss; our success rate has been good and we always striving to get better.

We discussed treatment options for milk fever, and I administered calcium borogluconate. Milk fever is not a fever, in the real sense of the word, but is brought on by a calcium deficiency. The ewe depletes her body for her lambs. She did make a full recovery, so we think we got it right this time.

We then set about docking the lambs, which is banding the tails, with a rubber band that looks like a life saver candy, for hygiene. This causes the tail to die and fall off. Then we weigh the lambs to determine if they have gained enough weight to be turned out. Then, it's up to the house for record keeping.

I have learned over the years that keeping records and notes is well worth the time spent. Often a problem will come up and you ask yourself, "Haven't we seen this before?" It also gives us a yardstick to measure lamb progress and gain. Our normal rule of thumb is to keep ewes and lambs in a jug (shepherd's term for a bedded pen), for three days.

We weigh them at birth. Then dip, strip, and check their condition and attitude. Are they lively and active? Lambs will normally be on their feet, albeit shakily, within the first half-hour. They are guided through natural instinct to start looking for that first meal. It is humorous to watch them poking their little noses into all parts of the ewe's underside, as if to say, "I know there's something I should be looking for, somewhere here." When we see them get it right and get connected with the mother ship, the little tails start going a mile a minute. Then we smile and the world is good.

Dipping consists of dipping the lamb's umbilical cord in strong iodine to ward off infection, as the cord is still open. Stripping involves checking the ewe's udder, to make sure it is soft, gently testing each tit to make sure she is milking. Usually the tit contains a waxy plug provided by nature to seal it until needed. The lamb normally can get the flow started, but just to make sure it goes as easy as possible, we strip, which involves hand milking a few drops from each tit to make sure it flows.

If after three days we have recorded a weight gain, they can be turned out.

We generally expect to see a gain of at least a pound. Anything less is a flag. Perhaps they are a triplet, and are not getting their share. If any are not showing what we would expect them to gain, they stay in, under close watch. Finally, last bed check before we turn in for the night. We'll walk the pasture looking for problems and check the barn.

Was today typical? I think there is no such thing as a typical day!

LAWN LAMBS

It is Tuesday. Graham decides he wants to take some lambs to auction. He wants to know if George can help him load lambs. "No", I say, "I will help you. George needs to stay focused on his studies."

So, off to the barn I go to help load lambs. No problem. I note that Graham is using his "new" truck for this task. He has taken the livestock rack from our usual farm truck and put it in the new truck. He has put cardboard on the floor, since the liner in this truck is plastic and deeply ribbed, just too slippery for lambs. All seems ok, but if I recall, this livestock rack doesn't quite fit this truck.

We load the lambs. I close the livestock gate and prepare to close the tailgate, when Graham yells from the cab of the truck, "Don't close the tailgate! The tailgate will just come off since the livestock rack is too big."

He sees the concern in my eyes. "Oh, it will be all right. The lambs can't get out." I hop on the tailgate for a ride up the hill to the pasture fence. The lambs push against the gate; not to get out, but because we are going slightly uphill. We stop at the pasture gate and I hop out to unlock the gate. "Graham, the sheep were pushing against the livestock fencing the rack was fabricated from." "It will be fine." So, I unlocked the gate, watched him drive down the drive, thinking, "Oh, he'll be alright. He can handle it," or something to that effect. Then I let the concern leave my mind and went in the house.

George was working on his math and I thought this was a great time to show him a game, online, that would strengthen those skills. So, he and I went online to play this game. I left George to this and I continued my day of dishes, floors, and the usual household chores.

Suddenly, Graham bursts in the garage door. "I have a crisis!"

I stop and look at him, as he is wild eyed and out of breath. George comes running into the kitchen. Graham begins to describe his calamity.

“I was driving down Bachman Valley Road, when I looked in the rearview mirror, and the livestock rack just lifted up and out! I thought, perhaps if I was quick enough, I could keep the lambs in the bed of the truck if I quickly stopped and shut the tailgate. I pulled in a driveway, and before I was out of the cab, the lambs were out and grazing on someone's lush front lawn. At that point I watched an SUV run over the livestock rack. I tried calling home, but the line was busy. I decided to go to the front door of the home. The lambs followed me up to the door. I noticed that the double car garage was open. Perhaps I could use that to corral the lambs. But, no one was home. So, I came home to get you to help!”

George, will you go down and get a tub of feed and the crook. I'll get twine. I guess we will need to hog tie them. You need to take George since I have no extra room in the cab. This will be disappointing to George, this as it turned out helped to save the day, but hey, life dictates!

Before long we were off. George is in the car with me and we are following Graham, who is speeding down Bachman

Valley Rd. Both George and I are looking for loose lambs. Then Graham turns around and heads toward home. Again, George and I are searching frantically. When we are almost back at our road, George calls his father on the cell phone to see what is going on. In Graham's panic, he doesn't know where he lost the lambs. So, we are turning around and going back down Bachman Valley Road, searching.

Of course, my mind is calling the Humane Society and explaining to them that we have lost three lambs.

Finally, George and I see Graham's truck in a driveway, three lawn lambs happily munching, but warily looking on at us. The cars on Bachman Valley Road are zooming past at 50 to 60 miles per hour. I holler my concern, "We need to make sure the lambs do not panic and run toward the road. If they cause an accident, we are liable!"

Now, how are we going to capture three 100-pound lambs? Graham puts the feed tub out. One lamb is piggish enough to check it out and begin munching. Graham lunged for her and executed a wonderful capture. He pulled out the twine and tied her legs up like you see them do with calves in a rodeo. As he picks her up to put her in the back of the truck, the other lambs panic! My thought returns to the zooming traffic, "No, don't put her in the truck! The other lambs are panicking!" So, then what am I to do? Graham retorts as he wearily returns the lamb to the feed tub, keeping a death grip on her. "I am not sure...."

George gets a handful of grain and quietly begins begging a lamb to come near. I begin to tie up Graham's captured lamb. As I finish, George hollers, "I have one!" I quickly jump up and run to him with the twine, to begin tying that one's legs. Before I am finished tying off this lamb, Graham yells that he has the other. This third lamb had come over to nose the tied up lamb, and Graham was able to grab her.

Once all the lambs were hog-tied and in the truck, Graham pleads, "Will you follow me to the auction, just in case?" I am thinking, "In case of what? The lambs untie themselves, jump out and fall into my windshield?"

So, we are off. We only have about 6-7 miles to the auction house. About 2 miles into our journey, George says warily, "Mom, something is wrong with Dad's front end." Then he begins describing to me how the right front tire is angled out. He asks, "Mom, can you pull over to the right so I can see, better?"

"His right front tire is almost flat!", and with that George is on the cell phone. He tells his father who apparently replies that he can make it to the auction. We stop at a red light. George jumps out of the car and is sprinting toward his Father's truck. His arms are waving and he is pointing toward the station on our left, which has an air hose.

The light changes to green, Graham swings left across lanes. George gets in the car, and I, too, cut across some lanes. We pull into the station, but Graham is clueless on where the air hose is. We flag him over to the area. George stays at the pump and I park the car out of the way.

As I walk toward the truck, George is filling the tire. "Dad, I can hear the air coming out!"

Graham replies, “It’s okay, George, just fill it. We can make it to the auction" George says, "Dad, just feel the air right here, Dad, just feel the air."

I am hoping Graham is right, but if not, well, better we know it now!

I see the lambs hog-tied in the back. I just hope no one is looking and thinking horrible thoughts.

"I'll see if I have Fix-A-Flat or something in my trunk." I leave not knowing if I do or not. Not. I run to the store to check their auto supplies. Windshield wiper fluid, oil, transmission fluid. I must have missed it. I check again. Air fresheners, oil, and transmission fluid. No Fix-A-Flat!

As I return to the staging area, Graham is searching through his truck wildly. George is still standing there with the air hose. "Nothing to help us in the store or my trunk!" I report. Graham rights himself with a smile. In his hand is a sheet metal screw. He screws the screw into the hole of the tire, which gives you an idea of how large of a hole it was! He said something about redneck tire repair! George pumps up the tire. The screw holds!

We all scramble back into our vehicles to continue our adventure from Hell. All of us were pleased to make it to the auction and home again without further ado. Admittedly, we had a tire to fix after we arrived home, but hey, after our day, that was easy.

VOICES

To most people the sound a sheep makes is a baa! When you've been around them as long as we have, you learn they do have distinct differences in their voices. There is a different vocabulary used by a mother ewe calling or talking to her lamb. Just as I remember from horse breeding, the mare talks to the foal with a voice only heard after birthing. Many have a sound that is instantly recognizable to our ears due to long association. The sound ranges from a plaintive baa to a sound that would give due credit to a bull moose.

The loudest belongs to Dozen, who is mentioned throughout this book. Sort of a course raspy baa. I will always know when she is hollering, and will respond, usually, "What do you want"? Yes, we do converse with our sheep. This voice recognition is an aid at times, as a distress baa is different than the norm. Listening to most of mine they distinctly say maa, not baa.

Lambs, early on, imprint on the sound and scent of their mothers. It is a needed survival skill. Picture dozens of ewes and lambs milling around in a pasture. How do they know who belongs to whom? The mother ewe will call her children when she wants to know where they are, or it is time for dinner. The lambs will also call when they are hungry, if not staying with their mothers. The ewe answers, the lamb recognizes the sound and comes running. As they get to be teenagers, often the ewe's calls will go unheeded.

If she does not receive a response, they will often get panic stricken, and start to run all around in a snit. Probably most of us can relate to that scenario with teenagers.

The lambs also have a very plaintive voice when they can't locate mom. When we feed in the barn, the doors are shut until they finish. If a very young lamb, less than one month, does not come in with mom, panic sets in. The thought of being an orphan without that nice rich milk is more than they can handle. At times, I have scooped up the lost lamb in my arms and went to seek out mother. After the joyful uniting, I continue with my chores.

I have been alerted to a problem by being "called." Last summer in July, I was standing in front of the garage when I could hear one baaing in obvious distress. It caught my attention as they are normally relatively quiet in the evening as they are on pasture and are not being fed. I could tell it was only one individual. The sound was coming from the upper sheepcote, so an investigation was in order. When I arrived, the first impression was, "Oh shoot!", or words to that effect. Shoshone has prolapsed.

A simple non-medical explanation of a prolapse, the inside of the sheep is trying to come out of their butt. Picture in your mind a large wad of pink bubblegum.

When examined closer, as she was down on her belly, and dang, there is a nose in that mass. She was trying to give birth but the lamb's legs were back. The normal we love to see is two hoofs followed by a nose. Time is of the essence, lay down next to her, in the manure, I might add, roll up sleeve, insert arm. Time counts more than cleanliness, as if she has been in labor a protracted time, they will become physically exhausted and can't help by pushing. Pulled the first leg forward, good, good, good. Then in for the other. So far, so good. Check the lamb by gently inserting a finger into its mouth. I could feel the tongue move on my finger. Great! Looks like I made it in time. With a little gentle rocking motion side to side, and some assistance from the ewe, the lamb slipped out.

Went to get a feed sack to lay the lamb on, as where she chose to give birth was anything but clean. The lamb was covered with dirt and manure so a towel was grabbed, and quick cleaning was done. The ewe will start to lick and clean the lamb, no matter how gross it is with dirt, mud or whatever. We do endeavor to get them to lamb in the barn, in a nice clean jug, but sometimes they don't listen, or in this case, blind side us. Ahh, the power of motherhood. Uck!

After a short period of several minutes, to allow them to get acquainted, picked up the lamb and moved it to a section of the cote where we have a separate closed area. The upper cote is not usually used for lambing but where we herd the ewes that have given birth and been weaned. Also where we keep our other registered ram or flock ram depending on whom he will be breeding. The ewe will follow her lamb, so this is usually a very simple procedure as long as you follow two rules. Number 1; carry the lamb below your waist line. Sheep do not to look up to find things. Number 2; do not let her lose sight of you and the lamb. We have had this problem when we are bringing in newborns to the barn where they lost sight of the lamb. The usual result is they take flight back to where they gave birth, madly baaing, looking for the lamb. Short memories, perhaps they all suffer from ADD. Don't you remember walking out with us until you lost sight of it or them? Did you think the enterprise beamed it up and transported it back to its place of birth? Walk back after the ewe, with the lamb in hand, hold it in front of her nose and let her find it again, repeating previous walk back toward the barn. Remind self about rules #1 and #2.

What made this event unusual was this ewe had lambed seven months earlier. Normally once a year in the spring is lambing time. To get back to the original subject, I guess from years of association with them, your ears tend to cancel out the normal pasture sounds, and only pick up on the out of place or unusual.

When feeding time nears, they will all holler at anyone they see trying to convince you they are all wool and bone, have not been fed in years, and could you please hurry before deaths angel get there. The pandemonium chorus starts when someone begins across the pasture toward the barn. Then starts the circling the wagons. Like an old cowboy and Indian movie, they will proceed to run in circles around the barn to make sure "if" a door opens, they will be first in to eat and make sure not to miss out.

The voice seems to vary with the breed. As a general rule, our pure bred Tunis sheep have the lowest, saddest baas. It almost sounds like they are looking for sympathy. Several also have this kind of "hang dog" expression that complements the sad baa.

There are people who will vigorously maintain that sheep will learn their name and respond to it. An example that comes to mind is Twinkie. We would sit out on the front porch in the summer to eat and enjoy the weather. If we had corn on the cob, the sheep would get the cobs. When through, Debi would call out, Twinkie! No matter where she was within earshot, would come running for her treat. Full speed, ears flapping up and down as if she was rowing across the grassy pasture. Debi was sure this showed that she knew her name, as being the only one to come. To test the theory, on another occasion, I called out with another name, such as sasquatch. She would still come running, thus proving, at least to my satisfaction, that it was the sound of the voice, not the name that drew the response. Try it with your own pet sometime. In twenty-five years, have never had an instance where they responded to a name, no matter how many times we tell them. I talk to Dozen by name every time I see her. The only response received is that same blank, "Where's my feed?" look.

THE SHEARING

Shearing is a rather normal procedure that many shepherds do for themselves. Not exactly a fun task, sort of akin to giving a cat a bath. It is normally planned to be done in the spring while the weather is not as brutally hot to work outside.

As it came to pass a few years ago, we received a phone call from an old and dear friend. He proceeded to spin this tale of woe about a close friend of his.

Seems his friend, a World War II vet (who is crippled and confined to a wheel chair) had several, "pet" (for lack of a better term) sheep he wanted to get shorn.

Considering the circumstances, Debi felt she could not say no. She has a fondness for older men and a deep respect for veterans. I have doubt that there are many people who can shear who would have agreed to do the job gratis. So I told my friend, John, that we would be willing to go down to shear Paul's sheep for him.

Mind you this is in the middle of the summer with temperatures of ninety degrees or better. Most reading this may never have had the experience of shearing an animal, so let me tell you from the past; it is hard, dirty, and sweaty work. It is easy to understand why there are few people shearing, and they seem to get scarcer every year. All three of us have done it, but

Debi, bless her soul, is the only one who has kept at it.

John set up a date, and we met him at his house, as he was going to have us follow him. He wanted to visit, and felt the directions were rather complicated so he would lead us there.

Debi, George, and I, loaded up the shearing equipment and drove over to John's house to meet him. He led with his truck, and after what seemed like forever, we arrived where a small lane wound up into the woods. Picture if you wanted to kidnap someone and take them where they would be unlikely to be found. We arrived there.

The property consisted of a tall, grassy clearing in the forest with an old house. Poking through the grass was an assortment of things, for lack of a better term. Old vehicles, boats, trailers, tractors… you get the picture.

After a period of meet-and-greet, Paul explained some of the history of the place-informed us they believed the house was the oldest in the county. Much of the area around where he lives is now a forested state park.

Well, it came to be show time. They had confined the sheep to the barn the previous night, at our request, as it is not very practical to shear a wet sheep. Also, the idea of trying to chase down sheep, in the heat, would only make the job harder and hotter.

When we looked into the lean-to on the end of the barn, an area about 10x24 feet, there they were. They were fat. They were matted. They were dirty. They were not exactly petting animals. I truly believe sheep have some sort of early warning system, like ESP, that tells them, "Run! Do not let yourself be caught! They are going to do horrible things to you!"

By now we were beginning to have a gallery of onlookers to watch the show. Guess they were all family or at least related in some way. One I remember very clearly. Young man-I would guess in his early twenties- sleeveless tee shirt, basically skinhead haircut, tattoos up both arms.

He jumped in to help by going into the barn area, "To catch the sheep."

Throwing yourself at a sheep to try to catch it usually results in more face- down-in-the-manure and dirt than catches. "But she was there when I leapt... where did she go!?" After learning the corner, "crowd and subdue" method, and realizing we did not care who was first, he was finally to gain the upper hand and one was wrestled out the door, upside down, dragging it by its hind legs.

Debi, in her farmer's bib coveralls, took over the ewe from him. To watch someone do it, looks simpler than it is. It is not unusual for the animal to outweigh the Shearer. Watching her put the sheep's head to its side, pulling then over to lay then onto their other side, then sitting them up on their rump with their back toward her legs all in one smooth motion is...well, not as simple as it sounds. Watch any craftsman ply their trade and they can make it look sooo simple. If you do any task often enough, it becomes easier and smoother. The trick being more technique and practice than strength.

The same young man after watching Debi throw and work with the sheep, was heard to remark, "I sure wouldn't want to mess with her."

The shearing proceeded outside in the bright hot sun after an extension cord that finally worked was provided to power the shears.

We have learned over the years to work together as a team. You can reach a level where you can usually anticipate what is needed or to be done next. While Debi shears, I usually am the Shearer's assistant.

What that entails, I hover, like a vulture, around her to help.

If the sheep starts to thrash, as they often do, she needs both hands to restrain them. I grab the clippers from her hand to allow her to regain control. When control is regained, and she asks me, I turn the clippers on and put them back in her hand.

Another function of the Shearer's assistant is "adjuster and oiler" for the combs and blades.

One other very important task is keeping the clipper cord free and out of the way of the clipper blades. One time several years ago, the clipper head had a meeting with the cord. Perhaps it was tired and hot also, as that put an end to its work for the day. Only through rare luck of the draw, it must have cut the negative wire first, as it did not "light up" the Shearer, throw sparks or fire. It just stopped.

Where we normally change to a sharpened set of blades every third sheep, these-due to dirt-required a change after each. Cutting through sand and dirt does not do any favors to your blades.

At last the six were shorn. Paul and his family were all grateful and Debi flopped down against the side of our car with the admonition, "Please hose me down." Our good deed completed, we headed back home for a well-deserved rest.

BITS AND PIECES

There are too many daily adventures, to be politely put, that would not make a chapter, but begged to be included.

My loving and patient wife Debi suggested the title of this book, "Nipples on my knees." It comes from the actions of newborn lambs to try and nurse from your knees when you are in the jug with them.

Jug, is a sheep man's term for an enclosed pen, usually five to six feet square, where you can confine a ewe with food and water, while waiting for her to lamb. Also used when we bring lambs and their ewe in when they lamb outside. Allows us to monitor for up to three days to watch for problems, lack of weight gain, not nursing, any health issues.

It is funny to watch them poking their noses everywhere, and Debi will tell them, "There is no milk there." Nature teaches them to look, they just do not know where. My original thought was "Ewe and me" but liked her idea for a title better.

Every year there are some lambs that, for lack of a more appropriate term, try to suck up to the Shepherd. I must admit, more times than I would care to admit, it has worked and kept them off the truck. At times I have to ask myself if we are running a sheep farm or a petting zoo. They all tend to be my big wooly pets and are thought of almost as children. If you have a pet you know exactly what I mean. There are always those who will be hard to put on the truck due to the fact that they have given you their unbridled trust. How can you resist those trusting eyes looking up at you and not have a pang of remorse? It is not one of the better parts of the business but you must accept it. After all, it is still a business.

Years ago there was a lady I knew who raised champion show dogs. She remarked one time, something I have never forgotten, that you are either sentimental, or in business, but you can't be both. No matter how attached you become you can't keep them all and be in business. Besides, we would have hundreds by now.

The idea of naming all your farm animals may seem strange to some, normal to others. We do sell some of the lambs privately to people and one different approach comes to mind. One lady we know, who will remain anonymous as you may recognize her name, being a published author, always requested to buy a lamb with a cute name. Perhaps its name was cupcake or chocolate, or something equally cute. My guess is she would tell her guests they were having cupcake for dinner or something similar. Perhaps a little strange but who are we to judge? Judgment does not put money in the bank, sales do.

A neighbor of ours has a small cattle operation and a decided preference for lamb. In true old country ways, we use the old barter system where we trade them lamb for beef. It works out well for all of us this way. Harkens back to an earlier time where trade was more important than money and barter was the excepted mode of trade.

We had one ewe named Toffee, for her coloration, which looked like coffee colored toffee. The previous year she had lambed, but developed a condition in her udder known as mastitis. We were never able to clear it up and by all accounts she should have been culled. Being an attractive individual we had crossbred from a Karakul ram, she had beautiful long wool with a pleasant ruddy red color. Wanting to keep some of the Karakul breeding in our operation, she stayed. We knew in advance that she would not be able to nurse lambs and we would have bottle lambs to tend to, but decided to take a chance and kept her anyway. Turned out to be the right call.

She gave birth to twin ewes. At least that was going for us. We set up one of those covered gazebos with screen sides in the back yard lawn, with a large fiberglass dog crate in it and a fence around it. This facilitated our caring for the frequent feedings and removed any need for cleanup, as it was all lush grass.

As it turned out, the birth coincided closely with our yearly spring soup and bread party for friends two days later. We host a small get together where friends come to socialize and bring their children to interact with lambs. It is always BYOB. Which in our case stands for, bring your own boots, as February can be quite muddy around the barn.

The two lambs were properly attired in pampers and joined the party. The children loved it. We have many pictures of smiling children with a lamb happily curled up in their laps or giving them their bottle. It was a win-win situation and they all had a good time.

We do not know exactly why, and probably never will, why one lamb, named Nougat, died the next week. Both had received the same care and feeding. We have never cared to accept it, but statistically lamb losses are about ten percent. I guess in that vein, we are normal. Seems no matter how hard we try, the statistics get us.

One afternoon Debi and George returned home to find the gazebo gone! A violent windstorm had blown through, pulled it up from the ground and blown it across the back yard into a distant fence line. Oh my God! Where is Candy? She was fine…just waiting for us to return for the next feeding. She also got to spend some time in the house with us again. I'm sure the health department would frown on this but it creates less of a problem that most puppies. And at least they don't chew!

As with all good things, it came to pass, she outgrew the capacity of a pamper. It became time to move to the barn. She did not take too kindly to this as in her mind she was a house pet. We would take her down to the barn and turn her loose. Not to be dissuaded, she would return to the house to try to convince us that a mistake had been made.

She learned how to sneak through the electric wire fence without getting zapped and come to the house. If we did not watch carefully, she would run in the door with us. When she got tired, she would put herself back into the pasture and return to the barn. Eventually, she became large enough that it was not practical to sneak through the fence. The end result was ending her house visits.

I did at least capture some of this on video when she would come up and my son, and her, would have races around the house. She would play "Catch me if you can." She loves attention and has a playful nature. She was very people oriented. She might have made an excellent petting zoo lamb. She provides one of the more heartwarming chapters in our ongoing life with the sheep.

Lambo is a different story. We found one of the ewes in the solarium in labor for an excessive time. When we checked her, we found a nose and some legs, but she was not able to give birth. The lamb was so large that it would not come out. We then proceeded to do what we refer to as skinning it out. This involves gently stretching the vulva with the fingers and physically pulling it back over the lamb's head. Once the head is out, the rest is normally routine. We found out why she was having such a struggle. The lamb weighed in at seventeen pounds. It was as if she decided to have a two or three-week old lamb. It was just too large to get out normally. She also pulled a similar stunt the next year. Then, to avoid further problems, she was sent down the road. We felt eventually we might lose the battle, so why tempt fate.

Dumb and dumber were a different case. The ewe had given birth in the barn and when I checked them, found the lambs very weak and cold. I called for the Calvary, my wife and son, to assist. The very weak lamb went up to the house to be fed to jump start them. Not wanting to remove them for very long, as this may cause the ewe to reject them when they return, returned it. Next order of business was to get them both to nurse. For some strange reason, they seemed to lack the instinct to nurse. We tried anything we could, including my laying on the straw next to the ewe while the family restrained the ewe for me. I would gently open the lamb's mouth and place the teat in it. They acted as if they had no idea what to do with it. If we could not get them nourishment from the ewe, the only way to keep them alive was bottle feeding them. I also tried putting another ewe with them as the second ewe had lost her lambs several days earlier and had never nursed.

From the previous year, she seemed to be willing to nurse any lamb that asked. This is very unusual, in itself, and it was worth a shot. Well, dumb and dumber had other ideas. They were not interested in nursing from a ewe and only wanted a baby bottle. I think you are getting the idea where the name came from. So, daddy ewe continued the every six hour feeding routine. After a week or two, I could stretch the times to allow me to sleep between midnight and eight am.

I am sure you all are familiar with baby bottles. Nine

ounces is standard. Where these ten pound lambs fit nine ounces per feeding is beyond me. They must be half stomach. In three weeks they were up to eighteen ounces each per feeding, and asking for more. I made them a little feed trough, and they started to nibble on sheep feed. At six weeks, they were reduced to twice a day, then once a day, then one bottle of half water, half formula, after I could see they were eating around a half pound of feed a day. At two months they are pests as to when I feed them. They would hound me, loudly baaing, and begging for a bottle. Sorry kids, you are now sheep!

Dumb was growing into a nice ewe, so I decided to keep her and add her to the flock. When she became a teenager, several months old, her personality was becoming clear. When I was in the barn feeding, she was the one who would be climbing everything, chewing on everything she could reach, and generally getting into mischief. I would admonish her with "You little dickens!" And so, since dumb is not a very flattering name, she became Dickins.

Dickins became quite spoiled. When I would come into the pasture toward the barn, she would run over and heel on my left side, walking me down to the barn. She would be accorded the honor of coming into the barn with me to make up the feed. She is quite polite and patient. This is not a sheep trait. She waits in the aisle way while I put out the feed. Her status as a favorite does let her eat first.

It came that time of year for the railroad to do their Easter bunny train again.

I decided to try Dickins as a petting lamb. I was sure she would be fine. She showed promise, as she tolerated rapid motions (you know children), being bear hugged, and all the usual noise. She was given star treatment and pleased many children.

The week after the petting zoo I found her down in the run

in shed, obviously in labor. Being home alone, I paged Debi and felt I had some time to spare. When Debi got home, Dickins had moved out into the pasture. I could see a nose and two hooves, but knew that was a problem. She is still not fully grown and small for her age at one year. The problem, besides being small, was both forelegs were bent back. What you want to see is the legs extended out in front of the nose several inches.

So I flopped down on the ground, inserted an arm. Grabbed the knee and gently straightened out the legs one at a time. With that done, I grabbed the legs. Then, with a little wiggle and pull, the lamb slid out.

I moved the lamb around in front of her head where she could see it. The normal response is she will acknowledge the lamb and start to lick and clean it. She seemed to care less. Debi picked up the lamb, and I herded Dickins back to the barn to jug them. The thought goes through your mind that this is another bottle lamb.

I returned to the barn about an hour later and the scenario changed dramatically. She was baaing madly and fussing over the lamb as if it was the best thing in the world. Motherhood instinct had kicked in. I would suspect that she had been in labor so long that she was spent. That was probably the reason for the initial lack of interest in the lamb.

It is normal for ewes to have a mothering instinct, but she carries it to an extreme. She does not tolerate the lamb being out of her sight for a minute. If she cannot see little Dickins, she goes into a hissy fit, madly running around baaing loudly until she finds him. Most attentive ewe I can ever remember, out of hundreds.

Being several weeks old now, little Dickins is becoming a teenager and inquisitive. He will wander off to explore on his own, and like typical parents, his mother gives him more free rein. She has gone back to her old self walking me to the barn to be first in and not being too concerned as to the whereabouts of little Dickins.

Mystro came into my life in the usual way. I was at the Maryland sheep and wool festival and came to a pen where a breeder had several red Tunis lambs for sale. Nice lambs, but I thought the price was rather high, so I walked on.

At the end of the festival I went back and after talking to the breeders, the price had been reduced due to lack of sales to what I felt was a fair price. Thus, Mystro became my new flock ram. He was a gorgeous red ram that would make a fine addition to my flock.

As he grew larger, he liked to playfully push on me when I was in the pasture. As he got older, he became more and more inclined to playfully ram me, not hard, but you knew he was there. Not unusual in itself, but starting to become worrisome.

He was put in a separate pasture with several young ewes and had no competition with my other ram. Perhaps he needed some competition to deal with other than me.

His first crop of lambs turned out to be unusual in that they looked like clones. Hard to tell them apart as they all looked identical. I admit, I was rather pleased, both with my purchase, and results. He was posing no problems, but his true nature had not yet presented. Now that he is more than a year old, the devil has come out.

He has my wife intimidated, to the extent she has refused to enter the pasture with him as he has come after her. In her own words: “If he attacks me, I will shoot him!”

I have dealt with it as much as possible and to the extent that to go up to feed, I will lure the flock away from the cote with bread, rolls and doughnuts that I get as day old throwaways from the local supermarket. I probably have the only doughnut fed sheep in town. At least I turn those doughnuts into meat instead of land fill fodder.

When I go into the pasture with my lawn tractor to do spot weed mowing, he will charge me. Being safe on the tractor, I could care less. He follows me all over the pasture as I mow. From time to time, I feel him "ram" the back of the seat on the tractor. No big deal.

Well, it came to pass, that I got tired of his behavior and decided to teach him a lesson. I turned the tractor to face him, and he charged it. It became a contest of four legs verses four wheels. We proceeded to have "ramming" contests while the tractor was taking the brunt of it. The plastic body on the front was beginning to look the worse for the wear. It now has many cracks and the cover over the headlight is gone. Several times I got him sideways in front and was pushing him sideways all over the pasture. He never showed any sign of tiring, though he was panting and had his tongue hanging out. When it looked like this was getting nowhere, I finally got off the tractor and wrestled him to the ground. I put my foot on his throat and explained to him I could kill him if I wanted. I have had discussions with other rams in the previous 22 years, and they have usually recognized me as The Alpha. Not Mystro. He's the most hard-headed and stubborn animal I have ever owned.

When I am outside he is always watching me. It's as if he wants to say, "Let's play some more." Mowing along the outside of the pasture fence where he is, he follows along on the other side. If I mow toward the fence, he backs up and pins his ears back, a normal posture of aggression. Come on over to my side, and we can play ram some more.

The problem will need to be resolved before lambing starts, as it will hinder my caring for my new born lambs. It will be hard to sell him to anyone due to his nature, so I guess the only alternative will be the meat market.

The next day started out normally with me going down to the barn to feed. At the base of the fence lay a newborn lamb. I asked the sheep who this lamb belonged to and no one raised a hoof or spoke up. I figured if I went back to the house, the ewe would claim it. I watched for a while and still no takers. I moved the lamb to an open area in the pasture near the flock. Still, there were no takers. I brought them all into the barn to do a butt check and see who looked wet, like they just gave birth. Not one that I could see looked likely.

By now, the lamb was cold mouthed and very weak, almost dead. Once again, I have to bite the bullet as I have an orphan again. This was around 11AM in the morning. I tried tube feeding, but am never sure if I have it right. The tube may go into the lungs, not the stomach, which will drown them. Did force feed with a baby bottle of double strength milk replacer and cod liver oil. I put in a cardboard box of towels with a heating pad between the towels. It's up to her now, I have done my best.

Low and behold, around 4 PM, that afternoon, the lamb climbs out of the box and starts scampering around the house. I can't express how much that gladdened this old Shepherd's heart. It’s the type of event that can make your whole day. I won! We all know you win some and you lose some. But you always do your best.

She now lives in the garage in the upturned pickup truck rack I use for hauling sheep and lambs and sits on a large steel sheet I use for welding, covered with a thick layer of clean hay. Tried and true, I’ve done it before.

(Beats tracking down to the barn in the cold, and makes bathrobe feeding practical.)

Decided to name her Ophelia, as that sounds classier than Orphan!

THE RAM

We learn, in life, some of the ways we get hurt. Being careless, being complacent, and assuming no danger.

I had to go down to the barn to get a belt for my lawn tractor.

Having a "petting" flock can be both a joy and a problem. Opening the barn door, at least to the sheep, means feeding time. They swamped me and pushed their way into the barn. Darn, well they will figure out that there is no feed in the troughs shortly and come back out. I had walked out about ten feet from the door when "POW", I got cold cocked from behind by my ram. Knocked me flat forward on my face. Lying there and looking back, I was eye to eye with him. The only thought I had was being powerless. Arthritis has taken its toll and I'm rather slow to get to my feet. If he decides to charge again, I have no defense!

I was able to regain my feet and rushed him in the barn. We proceeded to struggle, but I was unable to throw him down. I had one shoe torn off and grabbed a shovel to pursue him across the pasture. He did try to charge me one more time. Previous experience in behavior taught me that rams point, select their target, put their head down, and charge in a straight line. The trick is to play bull fighter and step to the side of the charge so you are missed. He wanted to kill me and I wanted to kill him. After much screaming and chasing, we called it a draw.

My stocking foot was hurting badly. I realized a trip to the house to get some ice was the next item on the agenda.

Our bodies provide us with pain killers that often mask the injury. And my foot was a case in point. I had a bulge on the outside of my foot that was the size of half of a ping pong ball. After two days of hobbling around, I decided the prudent course was to see a doctor.

Yep, they x-rayed the foot and gave me the news: Two breaks across the arch. Go see a specialist (with the x-rays) to show him. To make a long story short, he said it would eventually heal completely, with proper care, in 6-8 months. I tried crutches, but could not seem to get the hang of them. Fortunately, time heals all wounds!

COYOTE COMES A' CALLIN'

One morning, Debi told me, "There's a dead lamb in the pasture!" I looked where she said, and with the binoculars to see an obviously dead lamb. There was no real hurry to go down there, as you can't bring them back. So once again, coffee was the order of the day. After finishing the coffee and getting dressed, I headed down for a closer look. What I saw was enough to ruin any shepherd's day.

It was about a twenty-five-pound lamb that was eviscerated. If you are not familiar with the term, I will spare you the definition. You can look it up in a dictionary. My first thought was "coyote." We have never had a problem with coyotes on our farm, but have heard of other people in our area with the problem.

Step one was to call up the nice folks at animal control. When I spoke to the local animal control officer for the county, he suggested I bring the body to him so he could help make a determination. I thought they would send someone out to investigate, silly me.

I went back up to the house to get one of our digital cameras to document what I had found to better show the position and condition of the body.

I put the dead lamb into a feed sack and onto the bed of the truck. I then drove to the local animal shelter and took my laptop so I could show them the pictures of the condition as found.

The officer looked at the lamb on the tailgate of the truck and asked me to bring it into the back of the building to the holding/admitting area and laid it on the floor.

We chatted about it, for a while, and he proceeded to teach me how you make a determination of what killed an animal.

Taking a sharp knife, he cut the hide up the back of the neck so as to allow it to be peeled back from the flesh. He then proceeded to point out several trauma points, on the neck, which he explained were fang puncture marks.

Continuing his explanation, I received my lesson in killing. The tell-tale evidence could only lead to one conclusion…a coyote kill. I was given a short course on how you determine it was not a dog or other predator. Each species has its own particular method of attack.

Leaving the evidence there to be disposed of, with the rest, I went back to the farm to formulate a plan.

I was always comfortable with our fencing, as it was installed to contain the sheep and lambs with different types and combinations of wire fence. The bottom wires were connected to a powerful electric fence charger. The older adults would keep away from those wires due to past experience. New lambs would touch the bottom wire, bolt back, and after one or more encounters, never touch it again. They learned fairly quickly. On the times I had accidentally made contact, several thousand volts definitely got my attention and cause the air around me to be quite colorful with language that would make my mother less than proud.

One area, of about one hundred foot, had never been

bothered with due to the fact it was very boggy and overgrown. Sheep do not like very wet areas. There also was the remnant of an old wooden fence, mostly buried in the weeds, and undergrowth, from a time when the farm was a cattle operation.

Off to the local farm supply store for fence materials…

The quickest way to run a fence, in my opinion, is using "T" posts. Steel posts that you just drive into the ground and then fasten your selected type of wire. Posts in, snap on a specially designed standoff insulator, and run your wire through the insulators. Connect to the existing electric fence and have a beer (of course, that is optional).

I felt good until several days later, when there was another kill in exactly the same mode. Score: Coyote 2, Shepherd 0.

The next step was to contact Maryland DNR, Maryland Department of Natural Resources. They listened and informed me that coyote hunting season was 365 days a year. They said that if I wanted to hunt coyote, I should get a hunting license. What!!? Are they out of their minds? They did provide one worthwhile piece of information. They gave me a contact with a DNR listed trapper who happens to live in my town. Thus begins my association with Terry. When I contacted him by phone, and explained my problem, he agreed to come out to be of assistance.

He arrived and after introductions and him explaining what he recommended to try, my intro to trapping 101 began.

Terry is retired and only traps as a hobby. I suspect that for him, it is the challenge of man versus animal. He is one smart dude, who does everything he can to increase the odds in his favor. He boils the traps to remove human scent and uses bait that is irresistible to coyotes, beaver meat. He changes shoes to further limit human scent. He wears clean leather gloves. I think you are getting the idea…a total professional.

He placed several sets of traps where he thought they were most likely to be in the coyote's path. Three were placed in a triangle around the latest kill, as he felt the coyote would return the next night. If only one, which we suspected by the amount eaten, it would return on successive nights to continue to feast on my delicious lamb. To avoid any possible sheep trapping, I decided to lock all the sheep and lambs in the barn with hay and water.

Early the following day, I could see no trapped coyote, but the carcass was dragged about 150 foot toward the stream and none of the hidden traps sprung. Then, to avoid sheep getting trapped in leg hold traps, I went out and poked the traps with a stick to spring them. Score now: Coyote 3, Shepherd 0.

Another few days of spotlighting the pasture with a rifle by my side also proved futile. Another lamb was lost and the good shepherd is getting desperate.

One other method that was mentioned was the stakeout. Lie in wait for them. It was still quite cool, being spring, and sleeping with my rifle in a sleeping bag leaves me rather cold… in more ways than one!

A brainstorm! We have a small battery powered driveway motion detector that is very sensitive. A bird flying in front of it will set it off. Place the detector in the core hole of an upended cement block, aimed about fifty feet from the latest kill. Park our car just outside the fence aimed toward the kill. Place the radio receiver, for the detector, on the dash with the rifle at the ready and get some sleep. Reclining seats trump sleeping bags. Exactly as planned at 1 AM, beep...beep…beep. Coyote detected! They must have an alarm clock, as it seems that is their favorite hour to hunt, since all of our sightings have occurred at that time.

Before I could get a shot off, they got spooked and they

darted away. At least it provided a direction of entry. Back to sleep. Then again, at 3 AM, the beeping began anew. I opened the car door, and no matter how quiet I was, the lights inside the car spooked them, again. Back to the house and to bed until a better plan is devised. Score another point for Mr. Coyote.

Terry and I had walked the whole perimeter of the fence looking for possible entry points, places dug under the fence, tracks, and found nothing. Most of the fence is high tensile wire spaced about six inches apart, with the bottom one or two electrified.

I could tell Terry was also starting to get as frustrated as I am. Human nature endows us with a bad taste for losing. Who wants to get outsmarted by an animal? His mantra, is, "I will get him."

At the current time of my writing this, I have lost five lambs. Most of the remaining lambs and their ewes have been moved to my upper pasture above the house. So far, I have not had any losses from that pasture, probably due to better fencing and the lack of cover. The remaining three lambs and ewes in our lower pasture are being locked in the barn at nightfall, as that seems to be the only sure way to protect them.

Debi also has a few chickens and sells fresh eggs to our neighbors. Today she found one dead in the coop and informed me that we now have bait.

Never having done any trapping, as some of my schoolmates had in high school, I felt I had nothing to lose by trying. Any effort is better than no effort at all. I set my three borrowed leg traps around the dead chicken and hope for the best.

This is a side bar from another idea our neighbor gave us. They have two guinea hens that like to hang around our fields. Being about the noisiest birds that raise a fuss at everything, they suggested catching them and have a large outdoor dog pen they could be confined in with food and water. Set traps around the outside of the pen, should anything come near the pen, they would raise this un-earthly squawking alarm. Am considering this for "Plan C", or am I up to plan "Z" by now? I'm beginning to get so far back on the scoreboard as to lose count).

When I checked to see if I had caught Mr. C, I found a hapless opossum in the trap and the staked chicken body gone. The only trace was a chicken leg, still tied to the stake. Perhaps trapping is not my forte but at least now I know how to set and hide a trap. The dead opossum will now be the new bait, because, as I have been told, "Coyotes will eat just about anything and are opportunistic." Setting a spring leg trap seems easy enough, now that I am "skilled" after my first try.

I did learn a very valuable lesson today. It takes two hands to pry the trap open to set it. If you slip, as I did, and catch one finger in the trap, try to figure how to get your finger out with only one free hand. Seems I had become the new bait with the trap staked to the ground. Took a while, but was finally able to "un-trap" myself.

Perhaps the fence charger was not strong enough, so it's back to the farm store for a new one. I purchased the best and strongest one they sell. The label on the box suggests various units and recommends them by what you are trying to contain or keep out. The new unit purchased is listed for elk and bison. Hey, if it will contain buffalo it should definitely keep coyotes out.

Desperate, frustrated people often take to desperate measures. I stopped at the local gun exchange to inquire what they had available in inexpensive shotguns. When I explained my dilemma to the kind gentleman, he recommended a used 20 -gauge shotgun and buckshot. My thinking was it would be easier to hit a moving target with a shotgun than a rifle should trapping and all else fail.

The following night, about 1 AM, my son heard the sound of yipping from the front pasture. He got the gun and a new extra high power spotlight. When he went out front and scanned the pasture, he caught sight of the fleeing predator. He took a shot, which also caused Debi and me to spring from our bed. He was not sure whether he had hit them or not, but I am sure it got their attention. He mentioned that he had heard much yipping, which he felt, was Mr. C's intro to super-powered electric fencing.

Well, it's not yet the ninth inning, but the home team is still batting zero.

Time can become like a sleeping pill. Not having any contacts or kills for several weeks, we tend to get lulled into overconfidence.

Another of my ewes felt sorry for me and my losses. She lambed out of season for her, being the second time this year. Normally they only lamb once a year. That was an unusual event for us, but quite welcome. Feeling we had the coyote "at bay", I was not watching as closely as I should have been. We are all guilty at times living in a lull of false security. Sure enough, the lamb came up missing and was located killed, as were the previous ones. Looks like the game will go into extra innings after all.

Then, low and behold, two more ewes also lambed. Now the paranoia begins anew.

Being that we had not experienced any kills or problems in our upper pasture, we moved the ewes and their lambs there. Perhaps we are feeling a sense of false security, again? Only time will tell. At least we are still in the game and have a few more at bats left.

THE DARK UGLY SIDE

Unfortunately, things are not always happy, with fluffy lambs bounding through green pastures. Oh, if only it were true! All the books that we have read could never prepare you for the reality of life in the sheep business. There are moments etched in your mind that you would much rather forget.

That would be impossible, at least for us.

One of the first was Greyhound. She developed a problem lambing and we were at a loss as to what to do. It was very early in our adventure with sheep and is rued to this day. Looking back, I would suspect the lamb was turned with its back to the opening, not its head. The book tells you to insert a clean lubricated arm and reposition the lamb. It looks to be a rather small opening, so how can my hand fit in there? Being very tentative, I tried a finger. I could feel something that felt like wool. I wasn't really ready to jump in and left her, hoping that she would be able to work it out on her own. She died.

What do you do with a dead sheep? In winter, with the ground frozen solid, internment would be a problem. A scheme was hatched. If we tie her legs to her body we can stuff her into a large lawn-type plastic bag. To further make discovery unlikely, we inserted it into another bag, then another. We loaded it into a large garbage pail and headed to the landfill.

They have a policy of not accepting dead animals, so stealth was the order of the day. We drove in with the pail in the open trunk. I was attempting to look casual like any other householder with a bag of trash. It was quite a struggle to get the pail out of the trunk and dump it into the dumpster as she probably weighed around 150 pounds. All this, while hoping that the bags would not break and embarrass me. The plot worked. We made it!

The next time the situation occurred where we had to assist, I took the plunge. I felt that if we did not at least try, the results would be another death. Any effort, no matter how bad, is better than no effort at all. We always found that to be true.

The books make it seem so simple. Just reach in and re-position the lamb. Wow! The first time I did it, my only comment was, "What the heck do I have here?" Is it a lamb, her stomach, her whatever? Envision sticking your hand into a big piece of liver. The results that time were much better, as I was able to get the lamb out, alive. The learning curve continues…

Today we can say we know our sheep "Inside and out." It's now second nature, and we have all done it multiple times. I would estimate that intercession is needed about three times a season, more or less.

We had our son, George, doing it when he was about six or seven. He learned very quickly, and as his hands were smaller, we felt that would give him a decided advantage. He learned quickly, and has provided assistance to many ewes lambing over the years.

On one occasion, the ewe was in labor for several hours, when George told me he thought he should go in. When he did an internal inspection, for lack of a better term, he remarked, "Dad, we have a real tangle in here!" My response was, "Well, you know what to do." When he finally untangled the first lamb, it was stillborn. I think he was a little crestfallen, but I told him to not to dwell on it, and go back and see what else you can save. He was able, over the course of several minutes, to get two more out. Both were alive and kicking. His father's pride was very evident. When things looked stable, we retired back to the house for a well-deserved dinner. Two out of three, while not perfect, beats none out of three. When we returned after dinner to check on them, low and behold, she had snuck in a fourth one on us.

I had mentioned earlier in the book that when we bought our second Tunis ram that he had a dark side. We learned this the hard way, as usual. When it came shearing time, we originally hired a professional Shearer to do the task. When he was shearing our ram, Oscar (that was the name he came with), his shears opened a large cyst under the wool. We did not think much of it at the time as nicks and cuts are a normal result of shearing. Little did we know it, but we had just introduced the flock to a very virulent virus. It spreads mostly during shearing, where any cut can transmit it. From what we have read, the virus can live in the soil, also, but transmission would be more difficult. As a result, any sheep sheared after him, and nicked, could receive the virus from the contaminated shears. The next year we had several more cases of cysts. Live and learn.

The standard cure is to cull them from the flock. But being our only flock ram, the decision was made to keep him. We just made sure he was the last sheared, and that the cysts were pointed out to the sheep shearer. We also identified any others that needed to be done last. Or to be sent down the road.

I read up on the virus to learn what we are dealing with and found they make a vaccine to prevent it. It was being sold to prevent, but is not a cure. Everyone got a shot. It has taken several years, but we felt the battle had been won.

Low and behold, who should come down with a cyst? True to form, it was my Dozen. Being her special position as Shepherd favorite, she was accorded treatment not given to many of the flock…a trip to the vet. I drove her over and unloaded her in the vet's parking lot. She came out, looked at her, the diagnosis was confirmed. She has a cyst about the size of half a ping pong ball on the side of her face toward the back of the jaw, which had been growing weekly. The vet lanced and drained it, treated it with iodine and told me to cull her. I made it a point to ask her about the vaccine we had read about. She expressed an opinion that the vaccination did not work or was of questionable value.

Unthinkable! Cull my Dozen? Never! For some time afterwards, I had to treat and disinfect the wound daily being careful to keep things as clean as practical. I kept her up in the barn in a jug so we could disinfect the area where she was. I sprayed the area down with household bleach and water. After giving Dozen the series of two shots, she has never had another cyst. I've always valued and listened to other people's opinions, but the final decisions are always up to you.

The only other sheep that comes to mind having cysts that we were not able to clear up was King George, our third flock ram. He developed some beauties, in an abstract way. He had several, some as large as half of a tennis ball on various parts of his body. They would mostly go unnoticed, as his wool covered them, and as long as they are not broken, or leaking in some manner, the virus seems to be contained and not spreadable. It did not affect his ability to be a breeding ram, so the condition was accepted. By this time, we were doing our own shearing, and I took upon myself to do his. Over the course of several weeks, I would work on him for several minutes with a pair of hand shears. Tedious perhaps, but it was the best way for me. I would do this after they came into the barn for the evening feeding and were finished. He would just stand there and allow me to work on him. I continued until he had enough and moved away from me. It took about three or four weeks to complete the task, but he got sheared and nothing was broken open. Again, we have always been lucky to have such docile rams, at least from what we read about other people's experiences.

Probably one of the worst things that happened to a ewe, (I can't remember the ewe's name), occurred when we waited too long for a birth. The ewe apparently had not been able to get the lamb out, and by the time we interceded, the lamb had been dead inside for several days. At least that is what we postulated in retrospect. When we went in to try to extract the lamb, we found it to be quite stuck. The ewe had given up, so she was not going to be of any assistance. With Debi holding her, and me trying to firmly grip the lamb's legs, a pulling contest began. Pull, pull, pull…with no success.

Knowing it had to come out, I braced my legs against her butt and pulled and wiggled it harder. The result was not what was expected. The dead lamb tore in two. Not to gross anyone out, but the dead lamb had become putrid. Think of road kill on a hot summer day. For the only time I can remember, Debi got grossed out and had to get away to keep from chucking her cookies. Admittedly, we would never want to go through that kind of problem again. Sometimes it takes a stomach of iron to deal with life's problems. We then proceeded to extract the rest of the body and infuse medication to ward off infection. She survived, but the memory, and the odor, kept replaying in my mind for some time afterwards.

Martin, our Karakul ram, came to us from one of the Maryland Sheep and Wool Festivals. Walking around and looking at the pens of other exhibitors, what caught my eye was his color. Karakuls are normally black as coal. Martin was red. Already having a bias toward red sheep, as I do, I inquired about him. At first the gentleman said he was already sold. Oh well, at least I asked. When I returned later, and after a discussion, he thought I had meant a different lamb in his pen. Their price was paid, and being they traveled home in our direction, we arranged to meet them at an interstate exit.

Thus started our life with Martin. He did fine for two years until one day we found him down. He was not able to get to his feet as his rear end was paralyzed. We put him up in the barn and consulted with the vet. Being it could be one of many causes, she prescribed a treatment of various shots that covered deficiencies, and even polio. We rigged a sling to enable us to get him on his feet, even though he could not use his rear legs. His attitude was good, and we hoped he could be saved. Alas, after several weeks of treatment there was no sign of improvement. The time came to make that hard heart wrenching decision, to humanely put him down. A hole was dug behind the barn and his dispatch was done with a bullet in the head. It is never easy to decide these things, but you had to feel sorry for him as he could not move around and get out of his own waste. We had done all we felt we could so this chapter sadly closed.

Another occasion was when a ewe had just given birth in the pasture and something spooked our horses. The one horse racing around stepped on the newborn lamb, breaking its leg. Being less than a half-hour old, it was not smart enough or fast enough to get out of harms way. My son, George, got the lamb, and made his best effort to splint, and bandage, the fractured front leg. We put her and the ewe up in the barn and for several days monitored the progress. The lamb nursed and got along in the jug well, so we were optimistic. When it came time to change the splint and dressing, we discovered to our chagrin, that gangrene had set in below the break. Again, the decision was made to humanely put the animal down. This time George did the job, which showed me maturity beyond his age. I had offered to do it, but he said he was ok with it, and could do it. I'm sure it was as hard for him as it would have been for me.

While it is never an easy task to destroy a life, sometimes the kindest thing is the hardest.

The same horse also stepped on another lamb, but this time the results were more favorable. The leg was splinted, and the lamb recovered 100%. In fact, she became part of the flock, and was aptly named Crip.

We are now horse free, which, in retrospect, may have helped cause our coyote problem…who knows?

EPILOGUE

Many, if not most of us, reach a point in our lives when we say, "I can't do this any more." Sad to say, I have reached it. At seventy four years old the body's wear and tear due to arthritis has made even simple movements and chores painful. The result is the sheep have had less than optimal care.

I reached the rather heartfelt decision that I need to either cut way back, or quit completely.

I received a phone call one evening from a person I only knew casually from the hay auction. He told me he knew someone who was looking for some Tunis sheep, as he was starting a new sheep farm.

I contacted him and after some discussion, said he would like to look at what I was selling. He said he wanted to buy 17 sheep. I said that I was only looking to sell 11-12. We discussed money and he came by one day with his family.

Final result, I agreed to his numbers and he bought and paid for 14 bred ewes, one yearling lamb, one six-month ewe lamb and one of my adult proven rams. The money changed hands and he set about finding a transporter to take the sheep to his new farm in Delaware.

His bad luck started when they arrived at his new farm. One ewe was doing poorly, and I suspect she was trampled during the journey. He had the vet out to see her, but she had a miscarriage and subsequently died. One of the other ewes lambed and he had his first case of rejection. He placed the rejected lamb in someone's foster care. Welcome to the real life world of sheep that I have come to know so well.

Twenty-five years is a long time and it was hard to see that much of my life, so to speak, loaded into a trailer…and leave. Every one was born here on my farm and I knew them all well. They were my big wooly pets.

The gentleman who purchased the sheep owns and runs a middle eastern restaurant, and I expect that he will, within a year, be featuring local, farm raised, hormone free lamb.

He seems to be a pleasant person who I believe will give my ladies the loving care and doting attention that I once was able to provide.

At least I retained a small flock of two ewes, one adult ram, and of course my spoiled pet, Spark, who is mentioned earlier in the book.

I hope you have enjoyed reading my story, as much as I have enjoyed my life with my sheep.

ADDENDUM - THE OLD EWE

There was an old ewe that lived in a pasture by herself. She was a bit scraggly of wool, long of the toe and had only six teeth left.

As it came to pass, a ram escaped from a nearby farm and came into her pasture. Well, nature came to pass, and after the winter snow ended, she gave birth to a little ram. He looked up to her with adoring eyes and she beamed. He was of such sterling character, that the farmer decided to enter him into the local county fair. The judges were duly impressed. So much so that they awarded him the blue ribbon.

When he arrived back at the farm, he could hardly wait to show his mother the blue ribbon, which was proudly displayed on his neck. The old ewe beamed with pride that she had produced something so special.

After the summer, the old ewe sensed that her time was getting short and she kept her son close to her side.

One day she laid down and did not try to get up. As her last breath came, her son was by her side.

The old farmer came by to investigate, and then returned to the barn for a shovel. He dug a hole and tenderly laid the old ewe to rest. Her son watched and wondered what happened… but we think he knew.

After the farmer covered the hole, the son ran to the far pasture and selected the prettiest flower that he could find. Taking it in his mouth, he tenderly carried it back and laid it gently on his mother's grave.

The circle of life is now complete.

And she now roams a much greener pasture…

22329889R00065

Printed in Great Britain
by Amazon